Checkbook Democracy

Advisor in Criminal Justice to Northeastern University Press
GILBERT GEIS

Checkbook Democracy

HOW MONEY CORRUPTS
POLITICAL CAMPAIGNS

Darrell M. West

Northeastern University Press
Boston

Northeastern University Press

Copyright 2000 by Darrell M. West

Library of Congress Cataloging-in-Publication Data
West, Darrell M., 1954–
    Checkbook democracy : how money corrupts political
campaigns / Darrell M. West.
        p.   cm.
    Includes bibliographical references and index.
    ISBN 1-55553-441-4 (cloth : alk. paper)—
    ISBN 1-55553-440-6 (pbk. : alk. paper)
        1. Campaign funds—United States.   2. Campaign
funds—Corrupt practices—United States.   I. Title.
JK1991.W47   2000
324.7'8'0973—dc21   99-089243

Designed by Joyce C. Weston

Composed in Sabon by Coghill Composition, Richmond, Virginia. Printed and bound by Edwards Brothers, Inc., Lillington, North Carolina. The paper is EB Natural, an acid-free sheet.

MANUFACTURED IN THE UNITED STATES OF AMERICA

04 03 02 01 00 5 4 3 2 1

To all the hard-working journalists and reporters
who bring campaign finance stories to the attention
of the general public

Contents

Acknowledgments

I thank Bill Frohlich, executive editor at Northeastern University Press, for suggesting the idea of this book to me. Like me, Bill has long been bothered by our country's problems with campaign finance. His nudging persuaded me that a readable book outlining the recent history of money in politics would help educate the public about the controversies in this area.

In looking at the landscape of available books on political money, it became clear that no single volume existed that conveyed how recent campaign finance rules have become riddled with loopholes and why so many creative approaches to fundraising have emerged over the past decade. Relying on the outpouring of news stories and government investigations during the last ten years, I tell the story of how money has corrupted American political campaigns and why we should be concerned about it.

For their suggestions, I thank the outside reviewers of my manuscript. Their comments helped me avoid errors of commission and omission. The editors of the *Brown Alumni Magazine,* Norman Boucher and Chad Galts, inspired the "checkbook democracy" phrase. I am very grateful for their help. Frank Austin did an excellent job copyediting the manuscript. Ann Twombly took the book through the production process.

In addition, I acknowledge the support of the Department

of Political Science and of the John Hazen White, Sr., Public
Opinion Laboratory of the A. Alfred Taubman Center for Public
Policy and American Institutions at Brown University. I could
not have completed the project without the support of each of
these bodies.

Checkbook Democracy

CHAPTER I

Introduction

I T S T A R T E D A S a courageous act by a United
States senator from Wisconsin. Tired of special-
interest money pouring into political races, Democratic incumbent Russell Feingold announced a bold new electoral policy. For his 1998 re-election effort against Republican
Mark Neumann, he would accept no more than 10 percent of
his overall campaign dollars from political action committees.
Furthermore, the senator would stick to a spending cap of $3.8
million, roughly $1 for every registered voter in the state. And
the incumbent also announced that he would do all in his power
to raise 75 percent of his money from within Wisconsin and
would prevent national Democrats and sympathetic interest
groups from running any advertisements on his behalf.[1]

The system of financing American elections had long dis-
gusted Feingold. His strong feelings on the subject had led him,
along with Senator John McCain, Republican of Arizona, to
propose a radical restructuring of campaign finance several
years earlier. Dubbed the McCain-Feingold bill, their legislation
sought to outlaw political action committees, ban unlimited
soft-money contributions from large donors to political parties,

---

3

and restrict issue ads broadcast against candidates by interest groups right before an election, among other reforms.[2]

Early in the 1998 race, Feingold appeared a shoo-in for re-election. July polls gave him a lead of 49 to 30 percent over Neumann, a conservative House member with a record of controversial votes.[3] Voters respected the senator for his strong stance in favor of campaign finance reform, health care regulation, and education initiatives. They worried that Neumann was too conservative for a state that had a tradition of electing progressive Democrats.

Unbeknownst to Feingold, though, others had decided to make an example of him. Senator Mitch McConnell of Kentucky headed the National Republican Senatorial Committee, the body charged with dispensing campaign funds for Senate Republicans. A vociferous opponent of campaign finance reform, McConnell was furious over Senator Feingold's strong support for such legislation. In the party chief's eyes, restrictions on the ability to spend money represented a dangerous threat to freedom of speech and were an absolute affront to the First Amendment.

From his position as head of the NRSC, McConnell would make sure Neumann had plenty of cash. Money would be no object in the battle to unseat his ardent policy foe, Feingold.[4] If the Republican leader only could defeat the Wisconsin Democrat, he could drive a dagger right into the heart of campaign finance reform.

According to news reports, McConnell executed his plan with a vengeance. As the Republican political chief in the Senate, he redirected millions of dollars in party funds to Neumann in order to defeat Feingold. The Republican party donated $1 million to Neumann and spent about $2 million on soft-money ads criticizing the incumbent.[5]

Conservative groups also put substantial resources into the race against Feingold. For example, the National Right to Life Committee was upset over the senator's position in support of so-called partial-birth abortions. It devoted nearly $100,000 to full-page newspaper ads in several states criticizing Feingold's abortion views.[6] Groups that supported term limits and ones that opposed tough new regulations designed to crack down on the sources of global warming also poured money into the race.

Neumann himself criticized Feingold in negative ads claiming the senator, through his vote for a complex omnibus appropriation bill, had wasted taxpayers' money by funding a scientific study on "the uses of cow gas."[7] Another spot employed an elderly woman to say, "You gotta watch that ol' Russ Feingold. He's slippery."

In the closing weeks of the campaign, the senator was in serious trouble. The polls had closed rapidly. According to GOP surveys, Neumann was in a dead heat with the incumbent. What several months earlier had appeared inconceivable was on the verge of becoming true. Neumann had a good shot to defeat Feingold.

Hamstrung by his own pledge not to accept much political action committee money and to keep the Democratic Senatorial Campaign Committee from expending resources on his behalf, Feingold counterattacked. Out-of-state interests were attempting to derail his re-election, he argued. Neumann was a pawn of special-interest groups. Such organizations should "get the heck out of the state. Let the people of Wisconsin decide the outcome of this race."[8]

In the end, his plaintive appeals to the voters worked. By a 50 to 49 percent margin, Feingold defeated Neumann and reclaimed his seat in the U.S. Senate. The incumbent had beaten back a determined effort to silence his voice in national campaign finance battles.

Feingold's was not the only race in recent memory where money played a controversial role. In the past few years, we can see a number of new and creative ways in which money has attempted to influence the course of American elections.

- In 1988, Republican presidential nominee George Bush used an innovative "two-track" system of campaign appeals. His official organization attacked Governor Michael Dukakis of Massachusetts on crime, taxes, and the environment, while a second "independent" campaign funded by outside groups played an ugly racial card against the Democratic nominee.

- In 1992, interest groups opposed to Democratic presidential candidate Bill Clinton exploited a "public education" loophole in campaign finance rules to fund an "issues" ad claiming Clinton favored radical homosexual rights.

- In 1996, the Democratic National Committee and the Clinton White House took money from illegal sources, such as foreign nationals, in order to finance an early advertising barrage against Republican nominee Robert Dole.

- In 2000, George W. Bush rejected public financing of his campaign so he could spend an unlimited amount of money.

By the turn of the millennium, it had become clear that the post-Watergate reform system created to combat the dangers of large, secret contributions had almost entirely broken down. A "Wild West" mentality, where virtually anything goes, rules.

In this book, I argue that we now have a "checkbook democracy," a form of government in which money has hijacked the campaign process. It is a system characterized by large contributions, secret influence, citizen cynicism, weak public representation, and increasingly unaccountable elected officials. Big money tied to private interest groups has disrupted democratic elections, raised the volume of negative ads, and turned off the general public.

Checkbook democracy weakens the leadership accountability that is such a crucial part of our political system. The need to raise large sums of money leads public officials to pay more attention to donors than voters. Some politicians dangle the prospect of favorable tax breaks and amendments to key legislation in order to further their fundraising. Others look aside when infractions are made public, resulting in lax enforcement of current laws.

Even large contributors, who in many cases benefit from the status quo, are angry at this system. The Sara Lee corporation's chief executive officer, John Bryan, an early supporter of President Clinton, refers to campaign fundraising as "legal bribery."[9] From his vantage point, candidates spend all their time looking for contributions rather than conducting the people's business. "Everybody knows the system is absurd," he complains.

It is this legitimization and institutionalization of corruption in our political system that represents such a vital threat.

Charges of vote trading, favors granted, and unsavory fund-raising dominate American campaigns. Combined with selective enforcement of campaign finance laws because of confusing rules, voters, candidates, and contributors all face an untenable situation. Unless we confront and fix these problems, we risk the future of representative government.

In looking at the history of campaign fundraising, it is clear that money always has been a problem in American politics. Each era has handled the issue in very different ways, however. In the days before Watergate, our system of campaign finance had four basic features:

1. Weak disclosure rules
2. Unlimited contributions, which gave great clout to the wealthy
3. Unlimited spending based on whatever people could raise
4. Clear partisan inequities in fundraising: during presidential contests, Republicans routinely outspent Democrats by a two-to-one margin; in congressional races, owing to their majority status in both houses, Democrats outspent the GOP

Stimulated by public disgust with the Watergate abuses, there was a revolution in campaign finance in the 1970s. In just a few years, Congress passed and the president signed a massive overhaul, much of which was sustained by the Supreme Court in its pivotal 1976 decision in *Buckley v. Valeo*.

These reforms were based on four new features:

1. Strong disclosure laws designed to end secrecy in fund-raising

2. Caps on contributions at $1,000 per individual and $5,000 per political action committee, which sharply reduced the ability of the wealthy to fund individual candidates
3. Voluntary spending limits for presidential races in exchange for public subsidies
4. The creation of a new federal agency, the Federal Election Commission, with sweeping enforcement powers

Even more important than these legal changes in the rules of campaign finance, though, was a shift in the underlying norm of electoral competition. Although both legislators and justices explained their reforms as being mainly a matter of avoiding the perception of corruption in the political system, a perusal of the changes implemented during this period reveals a far more wide-reaching transformation.

For the first time in American history, the ability of the wealthy to fund individual candidates was sharply limited, although substantial sums still could be scattered among a large number of office seekers. And in the case of presidential con-tenders who voluntarily entered into the system of public subsid-ies (almost every major politician over the past twenty years except John Connally, Ross Perot, George W. Bush, and Steve Forbes), the parties were placed on identical footings in the amounts they were able to raise and spend.

This underlying spirit of egalitarianism was a stunning reversal from earlier periods of American politics. In every elec-tion before 1976, Americans could give as much as they wanted to particular politicians, and candidates could spend whatever they raised. If one party had more money than another, that was considered a tribute to its fundraising prowess. In the wake of Watergate, however, the risk of citizen cynicism was seen as too high to tolerate the machinations of fat cats or vast partisan spending imbalances at the presidential level.

In light of campaign finance rules before Watergate, it is not surprising that many of the reforms of the 1970s turned out to be porous restrictions on the ability to spend and the power of the wealthy. The combination of new court rulings, creative political strategies, and closely contested elections has led to a restoration of key features from earlier days, notably weak disclosure, secret spending, the presence of large contributors, and spending imbalances in presidential politics. Without any serious public debate, the 1970s' system, balancing freedom of expression, open disclosure, fair electoral competition, and equal spending in contests for the presidency, has been eviscerated.

To illustrate key features of our recent history and the more general problems of checkbook democracy, I examine a number of examples of campaign finance problems. My aim in these case studies is to illuminate various difficulties of campaign finance. I review how each problem developed after the *Buckley* decision, what the story says about our political system, and why the particular practice raises difficulties for American democracy. In detailed examinations of each area I discuss how accountability in American elections has been weakened and why money continues to be at the center of many of the problems facing our political system.

As part of my case studies, I rely upon press coverage, legal depositions, and government documents to get a sense of what happened. I examine recent court rulings that have opened the door to political abuses and created clear irrationalities in our current laws. Through open-ended interpretations of the principle of freedom of speech, many of these rulings have weakened accountability in our political system and elevated freedom of expression over other compelling principles, such as open disclosure and equity of electoral disclosure.

The outline of this book follows the general history over the past decade of how we arrived at this sad state of affairs. Chapter 2 examines the independent expenditure centering on the Willie Horton advertisement from the 1988 presidential contest. This illustrates how one major loophole emerged in the contemporary campaign system. Although the official Bush camp ran a "Revolving Door" commercial attacking Michael Dukakis's lack of toughness on crime, an outside group used an independent expenditure to broadcast a commercial using the name and likeness of the felon Willie Horton to criticize Dukakis. The Federal Election Commission compiled extensive evidence documenting that the two efforts were not truly independent, as required by law, but rather were coordinated. The difficulties FEC lawyers had in convincing authorities of this coordination opened the way for the flood of independent expenditures in subsequent elections.

Chapter 3 studies the rise of issue advocacy, using the case of the Christian Action Network. In 1992, CAN grew concerned about what it saw as the liberal drift of social policy in the United States, especially in regard to gay rights. Led by Martin Mawyer, a "pro-family" activist, the group decided to take action against presidential candidate Bill Clinton, who in its eyes favored "radical homosexual rights."[10] The organization spent $2 million on electioneering devoted to defeating Clinton, none of which was disclosed because CAN considered its activities public education, not direct candidate advocacy. Following an unsuccessful FEC lawsuit against the organization, dozens of other interest groups began running issue ads on subjects such as a balanced budget, labor, term limits, abortion, and global warming, all outside required federal disclosure laws. Today, more than one-third of campaign ads are aired by interest groups, not parties or candidates.

Chapter 4 looks at controversies over contribution limits through the case of Simon Fireman, a Massachusetts businessman. In 1996, he was accused of making contributions above the $1,000 limit to Republican presidential candidate Robert Dole. After pleading guilty, Fireman and his company, Aqua-Leisure, were fined $6 million; he was also sentenced to six months of home confinement, the harshest penalty ever imposed on an individual in this type of case. The episode reveals the schizophrenia of current campaign finance rules. Individuals, unions, and corporations donate hundreds of thousands of dollars to the political parties. However, because these "soft money" contributions are not given directly to candidates to support their election, the law places no restrictions on their size. Since the parties use such contributions to run ads supporting particular candidates, a clear irrationality has emerged in regard to contributor limits.

Chapter 5 describes the role of donations from foreign nationals to the Democratic National Committee in 1996. A year before that election, the DNC faced a serious fundraising problem. With Republicans in control of both the House and Senate, the Democrats' fundraising lagged far behind that of the GOP. Donors often prefer to give money to the majority party in Congress, because it controls the legislative agenda and committee chairmanships. Fearing for his own re-election, President Bill Clinton developed a fundraising plan that ended background checks on contributors and expanded the universe of campaign solicitations. The end result was an embarrassing Democratic scandal in which illegal sources were tapped for millions of dollars, much of which had to be returned to donors after the election. Even worse, thorny national security questions arose about whether Clinton's fundraisers had traded information to representatives of the Chinese government in exchange.

In Chapter 6 I look at the case of the Teamsters Union and the Clinton White House. In 1996 the Teamsters' president, Ron Carey, faced a close re-election battle. Brought to power to clean up a union that was the most troubled in the history of American labor, Carey feared his reform slate would lose to a faction headed by his archrival, James Hoffa, Jr. Seeking to guarantee his victory, Carey enlisted the help of Clinton's aide Harold Ickes. In return for assistance, Carey promised the White House the union would raise money for the president's re-election. By delineating the controversial relationship between the Teamsters and the Clinton administration, this case shows how large and powerful groups help government officials evade current campaign finance rules.

Chapter 7 examines the ties between big tobacco and the Republican National Committee. In 1998, it looked as if antismoking legislation had strong support in Congress. Scientific studies revealed a close tie between smoking and a variety of health ills such as heart disease and cancer. The American public had increasingly grown more negative about tobacco, with the result that smoking had been banned in restaurants, workplaces, and airplanes. But following a $43 million lobbying campaign, plus generous contributions to the Republican National Committee and key GOP allies, tobacco companies defeated the pending legislation and saved themselves billions of dollars. This affair reveals how large moneyed interests can defeat policy proposals that are supported by clear majorities among the people.

Chapter 8 studies the increasing reliance on non-profits, foundations, and tax-exempt organizations to finance partisan political activities. Such operations have become quite popular because they are not subject to disclosure requirements, have no restrictions on the amount of money that can be given, and can accept funds from whoever wants to contribute, whether it be a corporation, a wealthy individual, or a foreign government. With these obvious advantages, it is not surprising that public officials use these kinds of organizations as stealth vehicles in political contests.

After considering this range of money problems, the book concludes in Chapter 9 by examining why reform has proved so difficult and what we must do to improve our campaign finance system. The rules that emerged after Watergate and were upheld by the Supreme Court in *Buckley v. Valeo* are now in tatters.[11] Loopholes have been created that violate the spirit of the political consensus that developed in the mid-1970s. Today, thanks to soft-money contributions, independent expenditures, issue advocacy, foreign contributions, and the political activism of non-profit organizations, we have large amounts of virtually unregulated and undisclosed cash flowing into campaigns.

Indeed, the very terminology surrounding such loopholes is often completely false. "Issue ads," for example, typically have less to do with issues and more to do with negative appeals than do commercials sponsored by candidates, and many of them cross the line into direct electioneering. It is time for politicians, interest groups, the public, and the courts to deal with these new challenges and redefine the concept of issue advocacy. Issue-based appeals that are made outside election campaigns (and which do not deserve regulation) should be distinguished from "sham" advocacy spots using the candidates' name and likeness in the months leading up to an election that look just like political commercials. In the eyes of voters and other candidates, the latter are de facto campaign advertisements and should fall under the terms of current disclosure laws on spending and contributions. Similarly, tax-exempt organizations that promote specific candidates should have their exemption revoked by the Internal Revenue Service. There is no First Amendment right to tax-subsidized freedom of expression.

CHAPTER 2

The Willie Horton
Independent Expenditure

I N S P R I N G 1 9 8 8 , the upcoming presidential elec-
tion looked grim for Vice President George Bush.
Seeking to succeed the popular Ronald Reagan,
Bush appeared to be a long shot. No sitting vice president since
Martin Van Buren in 1836 had been elected chief executive in
his own right.

Bush's problem involved more than historical precedent,
though. As a man, he was a cautious politician with little vision,
and he inspired little public confidence. Moreover, the conservatives who dominated his own party never fully trusted the Texan
from New England. He was too moderate, too patrician, and
too boring for their tastes.

Facing him was a Democrat, Governor Michael Dukakis,
who looked very strong. He pulled off what was being called
the "Massachusetts Miracle," a stunning revival of economic
fortunes in a liberal state previously derided as "Tax-achusetts."
Early national public opinion polls showed Dukakis with a lead
of 17 percentage points over Bush. Some Democrats gleefully

debated who would earn cabinet positions in a Dukakis White House.

Underneath this state of affairs, however, lay a volatile electorate that would upset the conventional campaign wisdom and create a surprise outcome. Unbeknownst to outside observers, Bush operatives had organized a series of focus groups in Paramus, New Jersey, with so-called Reagan Democrats.[1] These discussions with small groups of swing voters were designed to test possible messages of the Bush campaign.

At the beginning of the conversations, the participants held a generally favorable view of Dukakis, based on his demonstrated leadership and accomplishments in Massachusetts. Slowly, though, the voters' sentiments turned more negative as key information uncovered by Bush operatives was revealed. How would you feel, the moderator asked, if you knew that as governor, Dukakis had vetoed legislation requiring teachers to say the Pledge of Allegiance at the beginning of the school day? Not so good, came the reply.

What about Dukakis's record on crime? During his term of office, the governor's prison administration had released on furlough a convicted black murderer named Willie Horton. While free, the inmate had brutally raped a white woman and terrorized her husband. Again, the groups' response was negative. The participants had not known those aspects of the Dukakis record, and the information made them feel much less positive about the candidate.

Within weeks, the Bush camp had devised its strategy for the general election. Republicans would attack Dukakis's record as governor of Massachusetts—the man was too liberal, not patriotic, and soft on crime. The Horton furlough was symptomatic of all that was wrong with Dukakis. Bush's campaign director, Lee Atwater, later would boast to party officials, "By the time this election is over, Willie Horton will be a household name."[2]

The only remaining question for Bush strategists was how to get their anti-Dukakis message before the people. If they directly attacked the governor, their campaign could suffer a backlash from women and men upset over the negative approach that could put their quest for the presidency at risk. Increasingly in the 1980s, the American people had grown weary of attack politics. Negative ads and tough rhetoric made the country feel bad about itself. Politicians who employed such tactics sometimes saw public support for their campaigns disappear overnight.

Caught between their need to place negative information about Dukakis before the people and their desire to avoid a backlash created by going on the attack, Bush operatives decided on a two-track system. The official campaign would attack Dukakis's views on crime and his record as governor. The electorate would have to be educated about the deficiencies of the "Massachusetts Miracle." Ads would be broadcast and speeches delivered emphasizing previously unknown information about Governor Dukakis.

At the same time, however, taking advantage of a loophole in campaign finance rules, outside groups would run a second political operation that was much tougher. This other track would employ "brass knuckles" tactics that would appeal to the basest instincts of the American public on the subject of race.

Unauthorized and uncoordinated, the operation would say things and run advertisements that were off-limits for the official organization.

As it unfolded, Bush's presidential effort would train a generation of political operatives in how to run a negative campaign. Its "two-track" approach would become a model of how to exploit campaign finance laws and use outside groups to deliver hard-hitting messages on behalf of the candidate. Over the course of the following decade, this strategy would become commonplace in American elections.

The Emergence of Independent Expenditures

George Bush was not the first presidential candidate to rely on so-called independent expenditures, direct spending advocating the election of a particular candidate that is not tied in with the official campaign. The strategy had been made popular in presidential elections by Ronald Reagan. As long as outside individuals and groups do not actually consult with the candidate or his staff, or otherwise coordinate any of their activities, they can spend as much money as they want to support or oppose persons running for federal office.

However, following the Watergate scandal in the early 1970s, in which substantial, off-the-books donations to President Richard Nixon had been used to finance illegal break-ins and dirty tricks against political opponents, Congress had enacted new laws governing campaign finance designed to equalize the electoral playing field and to eliminate large, secret contributions.[3]

Among the most important features of this new system was public disclosure. Contributions to political candidates had to be revealed in periodic reports filed with a new agency, the Federal Election Commission. The idea was that secrecy was bad for the electoral process and voters should be made aware of who was financing campaigns. Given the corrupting impact of money on politics, citizens needed basic information about contributors and expenditures.

Watergate reforms also imposed a $1,000 limit on the amount any individual could contribute to a single candidate in each election stage. The fear was that, in the earlier era of unlimited campaign contributions, wealthy interests had bought influence by donating hundreds of thousands of dollars to particular candidates. The potential for abuse in this area, demonstrated so vividly by Watergate, led reformers to impose a clear limit on contributors and to insist that wealthy persons not be allowed to funnel large sums of money to men and women running for national office.

At the same time, the playing field between the parties' nominees was made equal by setting spending limits in presidential elections. In return for accepting public subsidies for the nominating and general election campaigns, candidates had to agree to abide by caps on how much they themselves could spend. In 1976, for example, the first presidential contest after Watergate, candidates Jimmy Carter and Gerald Ford each were given $22 million to use in the general election.

However, from the standpoint of the reformers, one vexing problem remained. Legislation had to be carefully written so as not to restrict freedom of expression. Among the hallmarks of

American democracy were freedom of speech and freedom of electoral advocacy. Running for office and commenting on the qualifications and stances of one's opponents were time-honored American practices. Any restrictions on what was permitted during election campaigns had to safeguard constitutionally guaranteed rights.

Shortly after Congress passed its historic campaign finance legislation in 1974, a constitutional challenge arose. Senator James Buckley of New York sued, maintaining that the new rules violated freedom of expression. Because the legislation limited what candidates could spend and what contributors could give, he argued, the new law was unconstitutional.

Slowly, *Buckley v. Valeo* made its way toward the Supreme Court.[4] In its historic 1976 decision, the Court upheld the idea of public disclosure. Secrecy, the justices determined, had a corrosive effect on the political system, and therefore it was important for voters to know who was funding candidates for office.

Limits of $1,000 on individual contributions and $5,000 on political action committee contributions were also upheld. It was unfair for millionaires to be able to give so much more than persons of average means. For the Court, avoiding even the appearance of corruption justified this limit on individual expression.

More complex, however, was the notion of overall spending limits. Here, the majority of justices equated spending money with expressing one's opinions. Given the crucial role that freedom of expression held for election campaigns, several justices felt they could not limit outlays unless there were a clear and discernible social good to be obtained. In a compromise, the justices ruled that as long as candidates voluntarily entered into the system of public finance and accepted public subsidies, they could be subject to spending limits. However, groups and individuals who were not affiliated with the official campaign and who did not coordinate their activities with the candidate would be free to spend whatever they wanted.

It was out of this compromise that the loophole of independent expenditures was born. Groups that were truly independent were allowed to devote unlimited amounts of money to direct electoral advocacy because the Supreme Court did not want to limit freedom of expression. Candidates who voluntarily chose to accept public funding for their campaigns obviously could be limited in their spending; outside organizations could not. This decision would have remarkable consequences for later presidential contests.

The Reagan Experience

The first presidential campaign involving a test of this ruling on independent expenditures was that of 1980. Conservative groups supporting the Republican nominee, Ronald Reagan, made known their intention to spend millions of dollars in uncoordinated, independent efforts. They would attack President Jimmy Carter's governing record and extol the virtues of the GOP's candidate.

In their eyes, Carter was a disaster. Not only was the economy in shambles, with inflation and unemployment running far too high, but the incumbent was pro-choice on abortion, in favor of women's rights, and supported unpopular affirmative action laws.

Reagan, by contrast, believed in nearly everything they cherished. The former California governor supported tax cuts and a smaller federal government. He championed continued American control of the Panama Canal, which the United States had built, in the face of what conservatives saw as a treaty giving it away to Panama. Reagan sympathized with conservatives' social policy agenda on race, abortion, and equal rights.

Immediately following the announcement of the independent effort on Reagan's behalf, both Common Cause, a citizens' lobby that had fought for campaign finance reform, and the Federal Election Commission challenged the legality of the expenditures. They asserted that such spending by outside groups exhorting voters to support or oppose particular candidates violated federal rules limiting the amount any individual or organization could donate to someone running for office. After a federal judge rejected this claim as a restriction on the First Amendment right of free speech, the plaintiffs appealed to the Supreme Court. Deadlocking 4 to 4, the justices let the former ruling stand and in effect legalized independent expenditures.

A second major challenge to independent expenditures came in 1985. This time, in a 7 to 2 decision, the Supreme Court struck down a federal provision limiting the ability of political action committees to spend as much as they wanted independently of candidate organizations. The case involved two groups—the National Conservative Political Action Committee and the Fund for a Conservative Majority—that had spent massively in support of Reagan's 1984 presidential campaign.

The latter organization, for example, had funded a widely broadcast television ad, "Morning in America," which extolled the Californian's performance as president. The country was back, the commercial proclaimed. Times were prosperous and people were feeling good about themselves. No longer was the United States being pushed around by the world's tinhorn dictators.

By election day the independent groups had spent $20 million. Of that total, $15.8 million was devoted to supporting Reagan; about $4.2 million went toward helping his Democratic challenger, Walter Mondale.

When the case came before the Supreme Court, Justice William Rehnquist wrote for the majority that there was no compelling government interest that warranted a restriction of First Amendment rights. Justice Byron White demurred, saying the First Amendment protects the right to speak but not the right to spend. Paid speech was not the same as free speech.

These two Supreme Court decisions had an immediate impact on presidential elections. Freeing group expenditures from spending limits, as long as the organizations were truly independent, permitted large amounts of money to start flowing into the election process. Since the GOP historically had a stronger base in big business and among wealthy individuals, independent expenditures aided Republicans more than Democrats. Arguably, such spending could have helped the GOP win the presidency in 1980 and 1984.

It mattered little to judges and justices that the egalitarian goal of leveling the playing field by allowing the two parties to spend the same amount of money (and no more) on electoral advocacy was compromised through one-sided independent spending by outside groups. In this and other cases, the courts clearly indicated that freedom of expression was more important than equity in political discourse. One-sided expenditures would play an even more crucial role in the 1988 presidential contest.

The Bush Experience

Emboldened by Reagan's two victories and with access to large sums of money, conservative groups continued their work on behalf of Republican presidential candidates. In 1988, independent expenditures for the GOP ($13.7 million) surpassed those on behalf of the Democratic party ($2.8 million) by an even wider margin than before. Not only did such spending give George Bush a financial advantage, but it provided a strategic benefit that yielded massive dividends for him.

Presidential elections were coming to be dominated by television advertising; Reagan had swept to victory in 1980 and 1984 in no small part through the power of electronic advocacy. Nearly two-thirds of his overall campaign budget had been devoted to political commercials. Increasingly, candidates were discovering that electoral agendas and voter impressions could be dominated through a clever combination of attack ads and favorable news coverage.

Taking this lesson to heart, Bush operatives used the feedback from their Paramus, New Jersey, focus groups to develop a hard-hitting strategy against Michael Dukakis. The official Bush campaign devoted much of its energy and financial resources to developing negative television commercials and news coverage skewering Dukakis's record on crime, taxes, and the environment, among other things.

For example, an ad known as "Boston Harbor" maligned the governor's stated claims to be a strong environmentalist. One of the things Bush, a former oil-state congressman, was most worried about was his own weakness in this area. He had never argued very strenuously on behalf of conservation and had often supported legislation designed to weaken public protections. On the surface, Dukakis appeared to have a significant edge.

Yet Bush's commercial attacked the heart of this claim. If the governor of Massachusetts was such a strong environmentalist, the ad asked, why was Boston Harbor so polluted? Featuring images of garbage floating in the harbor, the television spot undermined a possible Dukakis strength and in the process defused what could have been a troublesome issue for the vice president.[5]

The centerpiece of this attack strategy, though, was the furlough of Willie Horton. From September 21 to October 4, 1988, the hawkish National Security Political Action Committee (NSPAC) and its Americans for Bush division broadcast an ad about Horton entitled "Weekend Passes" that criticized Dukakis's record on fighting crime. Headed by Admiral Thomas Moorer, former chairman of the Joint Chiefs of Staff, the NSPAC was devoted to promoting Republican candidates who promised a strong military defense, firm moral values, and tough crime laws.

Their first commercial did not use the menacing mug shot

of Horton that made him look, in the eyes of the ad's creator, Larry McCarthy, like "every suburban mother's greatest fear."[6] That picture might arouse the ire of network censors, who could refuse to run controversial ads by independent groups. However, after the spot cleared media scrutiny, McCarthy quietly substituted a second version that graphically cited the Horton case and used the mug shot of the felon that has since become notorious.

The commercial was a classic attack ad. It opened with contrasting pictures of Bush (smiling) and Dukakis (looking grim) while the announcer intoned, "Bush and Dukakis on crime."[7] The spot contrasted the vice president's support for the death penalty with Dukakis's opposition and pointed out that the Massachusetts governor "allowed first-degree murderers to have weekend passes from prison."

Next, the threatening-looking mug shot of Horton appeared on the screen. The announcer informed viewers that he had murdered a teenager in a robbery and that, despite a life sentence, he had received a weekend pass from prison. While on one of his ten such furloughs, Horton had kidnapped a young couple, stabbed the man, and repeatedly raped his wife. Then came the punchline: "Weekend prison passes. Dukakis on crime."

On September 22 and in the days following, news stories began appearing that told the tragic tale of Angie and Clifford Barnes, the woman raped and the man assaulted by Horton. While on leave from a Massachusetts prison, he had broken into their house. According to the victims, for twelve hours Clifford Barnes was "beaten, slashed, and terrorized" and Angie Barnes was raped.

After several weeks of blanketing the nation with the Horton story, the official Bush campaign started broadcasting its "Revolving Door" ad on October 5, one day after "Weekend Passes" ended its run. Scripted by the Bush media advisor Roger Ailes, the commercial made no specific mention of Horton, nor did it show a photo of the felon. But it reiterated the point that Governor Dukakis was soft on crime and had a lenient furlough policy. Accompanying visual images of prison inmates slowly moving into and out of a revolving gate, the voice-over proclaimed that "Dukakis had vetoed the death penalty and given furloughs to 'first-degree murderers not eligible for parole. While out, many committed other crimes like kidnapping and rape.' "[8]

October news stories about the "Revolving Door" ad explicitly mentioned that Clifford Barnes and the sister of the young man murdered by Horton were embarked on a nationwide speaking tour that passed through Illinois, Texas, California, and New York, among other vote-rich states. Most of these articles did not point out that the $2 million tour was funded by a pro-Bush independent group known as the Committee for the Presidency. Clifford Barnes also was a guest on a number of television talk shows, such as those starring Oprah Winfrey and Geraldo Rivera.

Shortly thereafter, a political action committee broadcast two "victim" ads. Speaking into the camera, Clifford Barnes told the story of the rape and assault, and complained, "Mike Dukakis and Willie Horton changed our lives forever. . . . We are worried people don't know enough about Mike Dukakis."

For her part, the murdered youth's sister argued that "Governor Dukakis's liberal furlough experiments failed. We are all victims. First, Dukakis let killers out of prison. He also vetoed the death penalty. Willie Horton stabbed my teenage brother nineteen times. Joey died. Horton was sentenced to life without parole, but Dukakis gave him furlough. He never returned. Horton went on to rape and torture others. I worry that people here don't know enough about Dukakis's record."

The Electoral Consequences of Willie Horton

This strategy was remarkably effective for Bush. Observers hailed it as a textbook example of attack campaigning. The Republican candidate got most of the advantages of taking the offensive (such as pinning negative impressions on his opponent) without suffering much of a backlash. For example, CBS News/ New York Times surveys revealed that until the last week of the campaign as many people blamed Dukakis as Bush for the negative tone of the contest.[9]

One of the things that made the ad strategy so successful was the favorable free airtime that it stimulated. An analysis of coverage by the network in 1988 found that newscasts ran segments from the "Revolving Door" commercial ten times in October and November, making it the most frequently aired spot of the campaign. Overall, twenty-two segments from Bush's crime ads were rebroadcast as part of news stories, compared with four from Dukakis's ads. The deceptive information in the Republican's commercials was challenged by reporters only once.[10]

By amplifying Bush's claims, journalists gave the ads even

greater legitimacy. News accounts quoted election experts who noted that Bush's tactics were effective and that Dukakis's failure to respond was disastrous. Appearing in the high-credibility context of news broadcasts, these assessments seemed more believable than would have similar comments aired as paid advertisements.

Not only were these ads successful at dictating news coverage, but research also demonstrated their ability to influence voters. Women and men who said they had seen the "Revolving Door" spot were more likely to report an effect on their policy priorities. Such persons were more likely than others to cite crime and law and order as the most important problems facing the nation.[11] This result is also reflected in voter shifts during the course of the campaign. The proportion of those who cited Bush as "tough enough" on crime rose from 23 percent in July to 61 percent in late October. During the same period, the proportion of those who felt Dukakis was "not tough enough" rose from 36 to 49 percent.[12]

Effective as they were on the crime issue, these commercials held another advantage for Bush. They aroused racial fears. Owing to Horton's visage, made clear in "Weekend Passes" and network news coverage, skin color was an obvious factor in how voters saw the crime spree. Republicans had picked the perfect racial offense, that of a black felon raping a white woman.

Experimental research demonstrates that viewers saw the story as involving race more than crime. According to researchers, the ad "mobilized whites' racial prejudice, not their worries about crime."[13] Viewers became much more likely to feel negatively about blacks in general after having heard the details of the case. It was an attack strategy that worked well on several different levels for Republicans.

The Question of Coordination

From the standpoint of campaign finance rules, the most interesting issue during the aftermath of the 1988 presidential contest was whether the two-track Bush strategy had broken the law on independent expenditures. In perspective, it was clear that the official campaign and outside political action committees had engaged in advertising and news-shaping tactics that dovetailed very nicely.

The first Horton commercial had been run by the independent group Americans for Bush. When the Bush media advisor Roger Ailes put together his own crime ad, he was careful not to mention the name Horton or include any photos of the black felon. After Democrats protested the Republicans' blatant use of race, Ailes replied that outside group ads were showing Horton's picture, not the official "Revolving Door" spot. This gave the Bush camp plausible deniability and helped the candidate avoid public condemnation for racist campaigning.

Democrats would soon test the proposition that these efforts truly were uncoordinated. For them, the coincidence in tactics appeared far too convenient to have been accidental. Using federal campaign rules as their guide, the Ohio Democratic party and a group called Black Elected Democrats for Ohio lodged a complaint with the Federal Election Commission alleging that the National Security Political Action Committee, the parent group of Americans for Bush, had broken the law on independent expenditures.

According to the complaint, filed in May 1990, the distinction between spending by the NSPAC and the official Bush campaign had been violated. It was legal for the outside group to expend funds criticizing Dukakis and supporting Bush's election only if the outlays were independent and not coordinated between the two organizations. Any spending that was made "in cooperation, consultation, or concert, with, or at the request or suggestion of, a candidate, his authorized political committees, or their agents" represented an illegal "in-kind contribution" in excess of federal limits.

This complaint led to an official FEC investigation into the relationship between the NSPAC and the Bush campaign. A range of top officials from both organizations were deposed by government lawyers, and a variety of documents were subpoenaed from each group. Several interesting facts were uncovered that cast doubt on the independence of the NSPAC expenditures.

For example, Larry McCarthy, the NSPAC media consultant who worked for Americans for Bush and created "Weekend Passes," was a past senior vice president of Ailes Communications, Inc. (ACI), the main media consultant for the Bush campaign. According to an affidavit filed by McCarthy, he had worked at ACI prior to January 1987. After that date he continued to handle projects on "a contractual basis with ACI" through December 1987, at which point he became Senator Robert Dole's media consultant.[14]

McCarthy confirmed that he had several encounters with Ailes during 1988. Some of these were "of a passing social nature," such as "running into one another in restaurants or at airports." In none of these contacts, McCarthy said, did he "discuss anything relative to the Bush presidential campaign, NSPAC or political matters."

But two encounters were more substantive. In June 1988, shortly after McCarthy was hired by the NSPAC as a media consultant, Ailes called him on the phone. The Bush consultant apparently had heard McCarthy was being employed to produce political commercials for the NSPAC. He told McCarthy that "prior to learning of my [McCarthy's] relationship with NSPAC he was considering subcontracting with me to produce media spots for the Bush campaign." He told Ailes that he "could not speak to him relative to any matters pertaining to the campaign, including media or strategy, because [he] was on retainer with NSPAC."[15]

Ailes's version of the conversation was that he had called McCarthy to tell him "he had 'blown it' because the Bush campaign had considered using McCarthy for some comparative advertising. I explained to him that was now absolutely impossible because of his work for an independent expenditure group."[16]

The second encounter came in October, when McCarthy interviewed Ailes for a feature in the *Gannett Journal*. However, McCarthy testified that "nothing was discussed relative to NSPAC nor any of the media spots which [he] had produced for NSPAC."[17]

The FEC investigation also revealed that Jesse Raiford, of Raiford Communications, Inc., a former employee of ACI who was responsible for postproduction editing of the "Weekend

Passes" spot, "simultaneously received compensation from NSPAC and the Bush campaign, and that he had expended NSPAC funds for the production of the Willie Horton ad."[18]

These were exactly the types of connections that Democratic critics had suspected when they filed their complaint. The Bush campaign had gotten great mileage out of its claims to have had no role in producing "Weekend Passes." Both the content and the timing of that ad were the work of an outside group, Bush officials routinely proclaimed. Such a defense helped muzzle critics who felt the Republican candidate was using unfair and racist appeals.

Yet, despite the evidence of communication between the two organizations, the FEC commissioners deadlocked 3 to 3 on finding illegal coordination between Ailes and McCarthy. According to Commissioner Thomas Josefiak, who was the swing vote on the matter, "[E]xplanations of [Ailes's and McCarthy's] actions were plausible and reasonably consistent. Their conduct, even as explained, demonstrated some bad judgment that risked the appearance of or provided the opportunity for coordination. . . . However foolish or deserving of criticism, the brief, isolated and insubstantial contact between respondents' agents during the campaign did not appear to involve any communications that, by content or timing, could be said to represent coordination."[19]

Similarly, on Jesse Raiford's employment by both organizations, the FEC rejected arguments about coordination because he "performed technical tasks—e.g., organizing film crews, bookkeeping, camera operation, postproduction and editing work—for NSPAC and the Bush campaign, and played no role in any substantive or strategic decisions made by either organization."[20] In the end, a majority of FEC commissioners concluded there had been no illegal coordination between the two campaigns. In the eyes of the federal agency, the NSPAC's Horton expenditures were legal and independent of the official Bush effort.

Conclusion

Since the FEC decision failing to find fault with the Horton ad, there has been an explosion of independent expenditures on the part of outside interest groups and political parties. Featuring direct electoral advocacy of particular candidates, these efforts have changed the nature of recent elections. It has now become common for political action committees to run commercials, conduct polls, and sponsor research designed to affect voters' preferences. Candidates used to be the only ones to run ads at election time. Now, individuals, outside groups, and even political parties routinely employ independent expenditures.

The two major parties have become especially adept at using this technique. Since the 1996 Supreme Court decision in *Federal Election Commission v. Colorado State Republican Party*, the courts have allowed political parties to spend unlimited amounts of money funded by "hard money" contributions.[21] Unlike candidates, who are now limited to accepting $20,000 from an individual and $15,000 from a political action committee in any election cycle, parties can spend whatever they want as long as the spending promotes "party building," a category that now has been broadened to include most common election-eering activities.

Parties can broadcast ads in individual campaigns exhorting citizens to vote for or against specific candidates. In 1996, for example, both the Clinton and Dole campaigns relied on their respective national party committees to finance ads outside the spending limits of their own organizations.

Issue ads from the Democratic National Committee on behalf of Clinton blasted Dole and Newt Gingrich for cuts in Medicare, education, and funding for the environment. Meanwhile, commercials from the Republican National Committee accused the president of not being trustworthy and opposing tax cuts for ordinary Americans.

Both parties (Republicans more than Democrats) also used independent expenditure ads in Senate campaigns. In 1996, the National Republican Senatorial Committee spent $9.7 million on independent expenditures for Senate campaigns, four times as much as its Democratic counterpart. Much of the GOP spending took place in the last twenty days of the contest. Republicans won ten of the fourteen targeted races.[22]

For example, the RNC funded Senate campaign television ads in Rhode Island (and a half dozen other states) proclaiming, "Jack Reed [or some other Democratic candidate] is so liberal that he opposes making welfare recipients work for their checks. It's outrageous. Jack Reed has voted repeatedly against replacing welfare with workfare. That's liberal. That's Jack Reed. That's wrong." After the spot ran, the DNC quickly made a $47,000 ad buy in Rhode Island. Reed ended up winning the race.[23]

In 1998 the GOP shifted tactics. Rather than engaging in independent expenditures, it transferred money to its state parties for use in public education campaigns. These funds helped the local groups broadcast commercials tailored to the state in which the race was being conducted. This approach also had the additional advantage of disguising how much money overall was being spent on the contest.

As a result, when the total outlays in the last twenty days of the campaign were added up, the top independent spenders were interest groups. The National Rifle Association headed the list ($1,626,000), followed by the American Medical Association ($849,205), Democratic Senatorial Campaign Committee ($802,000), League of Conservation Voters ($751,476), Campaign for Working Families ($271,230), National Republican Senatorial Committee ($255,150), National Abortion and Reproductive Rights Action League ($234,872), Campaign for America ($233,015), National Education Association ($190,149), Planned Parenthood ($142,262), Democratic State Central Committee of California ($108,876), and National Right to Life Committee ($99,143).[24]

From our study of the Willie Horton affair, it is obvious why the practice of independent expenditures has exploded. This loophole gives the parties an ability to avoid accountability for their disbursements and to disguise the particular funds being used to finance electioneering. Especially when money is transferred from national to state parties, it is difficult to keep track of cash flows and virtually impossible to prove coordination between parties, candidates, and outside groups. Short of incriminating documents like "Tell Joe to start running an ad on

September 30," colluding on independent expenditures is easy and involves little legal jeopardy.

In the Horton case, for example, evidence of phone calls, past employment, and dual employment was not enough to substantiate the charges of official coordination. Absent some sort of smoking gun, it is easy for outside groups to informally dovetail their efforts with those of a candidate, thereby getting around spending limits designed to ensure rough equality between presidential nominees who accept public funding.

Such bending of the rules creates serious problems in modern campaigns. Rather than competing fairly for the presidency, one candidate or one party today often has significantly more resources than the other, due at least in part to independent expenditures. Spending of this sort skews the electoral discourse unfairly toward one side.

However, the independent expenditure loophole is not the only one we should worry about; many other serious gaps in campaign finance rules are part of the current political landscape. I turn now to one of the biggest of them, a new phenomenon called issue advocacy.

CHAPTER 3

Issue Advocacy and the Christian Action Network

IN 1992, A "PRO-FAMILY" lobbying group known as the Christian Action Network (CAN) was worried about the direction of government policy. The particular issue that upset the group's leaders was the perceived movement toward "radical homosexual rights" in the United States. An increasingly vocal constituency made up of gay rights organizations had developed an extensive agenda that included guaranteed civil rights for gays and lesbians, antidiscrimination rules, adoption rights, and allowing homosexuals to serve in the U.S. Armed Forces, among other things.

Led by the conservative activist Martin Mawyer, CAN concluded it was time for decisive action. Rather than sit on the sidelines, as many religiously oriented groups had done previously out of deference to the separation of church and state, CAN chose to go public with its concerns. Its battleground would be the 1992 presidential campaign. The Democratic candidate, Bill Clinton, was sympathetic to gay rights, and CAN felt it was important just before the election to educate the public about his views.

Using the television commercial "Clinton's Vision for a Better America," which aired more than 250 times in twenty-four major cities, along with newspaper advertisements, columns, and direct mail, CAN condemned the nominee for supporting radical homosexual rights. Outlining the policy stances of Clinton and his running mate, Al Gore, interspersed with pictures of young men wearing chains and leather marching in a Gay Pride parade, the ad concluded by asking, "Is this your vision for a better America?" The spot gave an address to which viewers could write for more information about the cause.

Most relevant to the issue of campaign finance, none of CAN's $2 million in expenditures that year was publicly disclosed, because the group did not consider itself to be engaged in electioneering. Rather, according to the organization, it was following the hallowed American traditions of public education and the exercise of free speech.

Because it did not explicitly advocate the electoral defeat of Clinton, but only criticized his policies, CAN claimed it did not have to register as a political action committee, disclose its contributors, or reveal how much money it was spending. The full scope of its political activities came to light only after the FEC sued the group for failing to take these three steps, as required by federal law.

In appealing to the general public, the Christian Action Network foreshadowed what has become a typical strategy. Rather than make campaign contributions directly to candidates or lobby them once they have been elected, a number of interested groups now take to the airwaves during election campaigns and attempt to sway potential voters.

On the surface, the public education ads that they broadcast look just like campaign commercials. The spots criticize the opposition candidate, generally in the weeks leading up to a crucial election. But because they do not urge the electorate to vote for or against specific persons, such commercials have been defined by the courts as falling outside the category of electioneering. As I make clear in this chapter, though, many of them actually are sham election ads in disguise.

What Is Issue Advocacy?

This term refers to public education appeals run by interest groups or political parties that promote a set of ideas, but do not expressly oppose or support the election of specific candidates. Under legal interpretations dating back to *Buckley v. Valeo* in 1976, groups are considered to be engaging in electioneering only if they run ads or produce material including words like "Vote for (or against) Representative Smith." Even though this doctrine rests on a single footnote in that landmark decision, over the past two decades that footnote has taken on a status roughly equivalent to that of Holy Writ.

In the Supreme Court's decision, the justices sought to distinguish three categories of political activism: lobbying government officials directly, which could be regulated; electioneering, which would be subject to post-Watergate rules on disclosure, contribution limits, and voluntary spending limits (for presidential candidates); and public education activities, which would face no restriction or required disclosure owing to First Amendment concerns about freedom of speech. In regard to the latter, groups would not be required to register as political action committees unless they explicitly used so-called magic words, such as "vote for," "support," "elect," or "defeat."[1]

The obvious problem with the distinction between the three types of activities is that there are many ways to urge voting for or against a candidate without actually saying so. Given recent advances in video production, it is possible to employ audio voice-overs, music, visual text, visual images, color, editing, and codewords to communicate powerful, election-oriented messages to the people. Indeed, it takes little ingenuity to produce a public education appeal that complies with the *Buckley* decision, yet still tells men and women they should vote for or against a particular contender for office.

The result is that a variety of interests spanning the political spectrum have figured out how to engage in electioneering activities designed to influence the voters without having to disclose their campaign efforts. The growth of partisan campaigning masquerading as public education creates huge opportunities for clandestine political action. Without any significant public debate about this change, advocacy groups have gutted the system of campaign finance that was in place for the two decades after Watergate. This has created a situation where political dialogue is funded secretly, to the detriment of democratic representation and accountability.[2]

The Case of the Christian Action Network

The group that opened the floodgates for issue advocacy was the Christian Action Network. As noted earlier, CAN took to the airwaves in 1992 because of concern over Bill Clinton's stance in favor of gay rights. Spending around $2 million, the organization broadcast a television commercial, took out newspaper ads, distributed newspaper columns, and sent out direct mail letters.[3]

However, nothing in any of those activities would have provoked legal scrutiny: any group, liberal or conservative, has the right to express its point of view. What made this case noteworthy was that CAN chose not to register as a political action committee, did not comply with federal rules on disclosing electioneering activities, and was not subject to contribution limits.

This failure to register as a political action committee led Democrats to complain to the Federal Election Commission that CAN was violating campaign laws. Following a government investigation, the FEC filed suit in federal court on October 18, 1994.[4] The case was difficult to present, because nowhere in the television or newspaper advertisements or in the direct mail materials did CAN utter the "magic words" cited in the *Buckley* decision. For example, the television commercial informed viewers of Clinton's stance on gay rights, showed pictures of the candidate, and criticized his policy views. But it never told them to "vote against Clinton" or that "Clinton should be defeated because of his gay rights views."

What, then, led the FEC to make the activities of the Christian Action Network the agency's first effort at enforcement involving interest group television advertising? Government lawyers argued that the medium itself created unique possibilities for nonverbal communication and the use of electronic imagery not possible with print or radio messages. Rather than relying solely on explicit words, the standard identified in *Buckley v. Valeo* as the primary means for distinguishing electioneering from public education, it was time for the courts to recognize the importance of nonverbal means of delivering substantive messages.

I was hired by the FEC as an expert witness to assess what was contained in CAN's advertisement.[5] In my opinion, this thirty-second television spot expressly advocated the defeat of candidates Clinton and Gore in the 1992 presidential election. It did so by employing the techniques of voice-overs, music, visual text, visual images, color, codewords, and editing. As a whole, these techniques conveyed the view that voters should defeat Clinton and Gore because these candidates favored extremist homosexuals and extremist homosexuals were bad for America. This interpretation was in keeping with contemporary communications theories that outlined using television to increase candidates' unfavorability, alter the campaign agenda in a direction detrimental to particular contestants, and change voter evaluations in an effort to influence the election's outcome.[6] There were a number of specific ways in which this ad was a de facto campaign commercial.

1. Visual Degrading of Clinton Picture. A lifelike color photograph of the Democratic nominee appears in the opening visual of the ad superimposed on the image of a waving American flag. His picture then is degraded into a poor quality, grayish negative. Clinton's eyes and mouth become dark and threatening. The consequence is to make him look bad. The visual degrading of the color photograph tells viewers that Clinton is not to be seen favorably. It conveys the further point that he does not deserve support. The change in color from a bright, positive image of Clinton into a lifeless, grayish image is an effort to weaken public support for the candidate.

The poor quality, grayish photographic negative of Clinton parallels a *Time* ad run by Bush operatives in 1992. In its ad, the Bush organization reproduced a grayish photographic negative of Clinton from an April 20, 1992, *Time* cover to exhort voters to defeat him in November because of his lack of trustworthiness. The similarity between the visual degrading of Clinton's image in the Christian Action Network commercial and Bush's magazine ad shows this to be a common technique used to tell women and men to vote against a candidate.

2. Colors Unfavorable to Clinton. The second visual of this television commercial has a clear contrast between a bright color image of the American flag and a grayish, unflattering image of the candidate. This communicates the point that the flag is good and Clinton as president would be bad for America. It tells viewers that the Democrat is different from you and me.

3. Music Ominous for Clinton. The tones and notes in this ad do not, like a song, have melody and harmony; instead, the tones set a mood that is ominous for Clinton. The music is eerie and has a threatening sound. Halfway through the commercial, the pitch drops down into the deep bass. This shift says something bad will happen if Clinton is elected president. At the end, when the picture of the American flag comes on with the Christian Action Network address, the music is less ominous. This conveys the message that America will be better off without Clinton in the White House.

4. Unfavorable Visual Images Associated with Clinton and Gore. The commercial makes extensive use of five different visual images describing extremist homosexual rights that are bad for America. These images are identified by the narrator as part of Clinton and Gore's vision for a better country. One image has a banner saying "Libertarians for Gay and Lesbian Concerns" accompanied by text saying "Job Quotas for Homosexuals." The second has the same banner accompanied by text saying "Special Rights for Homosexuals." The next visual shows men with their arms around one another on-screen, with text saying "Homosexuals in the Armed Forces." One of the men in this photo is naked from the waist up and has a rope around his neck; the end of the rope is held by his companion. A fourth image shows a screaming man wearing a T-shirt that says "Gay Fathers," with visual text claiming "Homosexuals Adopting Children." The final image shows chain- and leather-bound men.

These are all unfavorable to Clinton and Gore because they associate their candidacies with negative visual images of extremist homosexual rights. Showing such images of gay men while discussing Clinton's vision for a better America was an effort to undermine public support for the Democratic ticket. It conveys the message that Clinton and Gore are aligned with extreme parts of society and that viewers should vote against the nominees.

This deliberate association is in keeping with scholarly

research showing that negative images are closely linked with decisions to vote against individual candidates. Men and women generally vote for individuals they like and against those they dislike. If they dislike both candidates, they vote for the person disliked the least. Anything that decreases a candidate's favorability lowers voter support for her or him. In fact, visually associating unfavorable images with an opponent is a common way of defeating that individual.

5. Clinton and Gore Attacked for Supporting Extremist Homosexual Rights That Are Bad for America. The commercial assails the Democratic ticket on homosexual rights and family values. Unflattering pictures and texts associate Clinton and Gore with extremist parts of the homosexual rights movement. Pictures of gay rights marches, gay men arm in arm, men wearing leather and chains, and men wearing T-shirts advocating rights for gay fathers are interspersed with text and voice-overs proclaiming Clinton and Gore's support for homosexual rights.

This commercial is oppositional and uses graphic imagery to grab the viewer's attention and convey a message. It criticizes Clinton's vision and juxtaposes negative imagery with his policy views as described in the ad. The spot shows that Clinton and Gore are out of touch with America and unsympathetic to traditional family values based on heterosexual relationships. Graphic images of gay men make the point that the two candidates are supporting policy views that are out of the mainstream.

6. Visual Text and Audio Voice-Overs Criticize Clinton and Gore. The on-screen text and the voice-overs reproach the Democratic nominees for supporting job quotas for homosexuals, creating special rights for homosexuals, having homosexuals in the armed forces, and giving homosexual couples the right to adopt children or become foster parents. The ad identifies these policy proposals with Clinton and Gore's vision for America and says such views are bad for the country. Clinton's picture appears in the opening shot of the commercial. A voice-over then says, "Bill Clinton's vision for a better America includes: [text on screen] Job Quotas for Homosexuals. Special Rights for Homosexuals. Homosexuals in the Armed Forces." The ad goes on to announce that "Al Gore Supports Homosexual Couples Adopting Children and Becoming Foster Parents," with the text on screen proclaiming "Homosexuals Adopting Children." The clear message: Don't vote for Clinton and Gore, because their vision is bad for America. The verbal road map provided by the narrator knits together the audio and video aspects of the commercial.

7. Abrupt Edits Link Clinton to Negative Visual Images of Extremist Homosexual Rights. The sequencing of images also works against the Democratic nominee. His picture is closely followed by scenes of the candidate advocating extremist homosexual rights that are bad for America. The abrupt editing cuts create a feeling that something awful would happen to the country because of Clinton's vision of extreme homosexual rights. At the beginning the commercial looks like a pro-Clinton ad, with a color image of the candidate accompanied by the American flag. This quickly shifts to a parade sequence of yelling, disagreeable-looking gay men clothes in chains, leather, and rope. Close-up photos of the marches amplify the sight of their screaming and their generally unpleasant appearance. The frenetic jump cuts create a feeling that these individuals are threatening traditional American heterosexual values and enhance the negative tone of these scenes.

8. Issues Raised That Are Relevant Only if Clinton Becomes President. The ad describes Clinton and Gore's support for a variety of extremist homosexual rights positions that would be bad for America, among them job quotas for homosexuals, special rights for homosexuals, having homosexuals in the armed forces, and supporting the rights of homosexual couples to adopt children and become foster parents. Some of these proposals could be implemented by executive order, but only if Clinton won the election. Having homosexuals in the armed forces, for example, would require such a presidential order; Clinton could not issue it if he remained governor of Arkansas. This suggests that the commercial's purpose was to have voters defeat Clinton in the election.

9. "Vision" Codeword Used in the 1992 Campaign. As the ad begins, the announcer intones, "Bill Clinton's vision for a better America includes . . ." At the end, after reviewing the Democratic nominee's purported advocacy of homosexual rights, the announcer asks: "Is this *your* vision for a better America?"

"Vision" is a codeword explicitly associated with the 1992 presidential campaign, much discussed in relation to George Bush. The president was widely criticized for lacking vision and was the object of jokes about his self-proclaimed difficulties with the "vision thing." In the 1992 campaign, this codeword became a sign of candidates' not having a political agenda and not understanding what needed to be done after the election.

The Christian Action Network commercial uses codewords to communicate the message that Clinton has a vision but that it is wrong for America, that his vision is not in keeping with traditional American values of upholding heterosexual relationships, and that Clinton's vision should be defeated in the 1992 elections by voting against him.

10. "Quota" Codeword Used That Was Unfavorable to Clinton. A substantial majority of Americans view quotas unfavorably because they are associated with unfair special rights that have not been earned by the group in question. In his campaign, Bush claimed that Clinton was in favor of quotas. One visual text in CAN's television spot says "Job Quotas for Homosexuals." In this scene, the narrator identifies Clinton's vision for a better America with supporting this position. And then, at the end of the ad, the announcer asks, "Is this *your* vision for a better America?" Use of this codeword ties an unpopular policy with Clinton so as to discourage voters from casting ballots for him.

11. Visual Disappearance of Clinton at End of Ad. The commercial ends by reprising the picture of the waving American flag from the opening scene, but this time with no image of Bill Clinton. This scene appears right after the announcer has asked, "Is this *your* vision for a better America?" Clinton's absence, despite the presence of the flag that had accompanied his likeness in the opening scene, reiterates the message that Clinton's vision for America is not consistent with traditional family values involving heterosexual rights. The end of the ad is designed to undermine public support for the Democrat by saying America would be better off if he were not elected president. Like a red international stop symbol superimposed on a candidate's name or likeness during an election campaign, Clinton's visual disappearance at the end of the commercial is a powerful visual image telling voters to defeat him.

12. Close Proximity of the Television Ad to the National Election. The timing of this spot, which aired around the country in the weeks immediately before a national vote, strengthens the argument that the Christian Action Network was attempting to influence the election by encouraging voters to defeat Clinton and Gore. Political television ads that are broadcast right before an election are perceived differently from those run at other times. When a presidential election is being contested, and competing candidates and independent groups are airing commercials, viewers see spots with pictures of major contenders backed up by narrators describing their particular visions as political ads designed to tell citizens how to vote. The close proximity of the Christian Action Network's commercial to the national elections further demonstrates that it was designed to defeat Clinton and Gore.

Losing the Court Case

In the end, the FEC's lawsuit against the Christian Action Network did not succeed; it even had to pay the group's legal fees. Despite the various suasive techniques which, in their totality, communicated the message that Clinton should not be supported, a federal district court judge, James C. Turk of Virginia, threw out the FEC's challenge to CAN on First Amendment grounds. In his view, "[T]he advertisements at issue do not contain explicit words or imagery advocating electoral action. On the contrary, the advertisements represent a form of issue advocacy intended to inform the public about political issues germane to the 1992 presidential election. Therefore, the advertisements are fully protected as 'political speech' under the First Amendment. Their financing is not governed by FECA [the Federal Election Campaign Act] and the FEC lacks jurisdiction to bring this suit."[7]

Judge Turk argued that nowhere did the ads specifically mention the November election, tell people they should vote, or ask them to cast a ballot against Clinton. The commercial's electronic imagery was vague enough so that different persons could draw different messages from the spot. Whereas some might see it as instructing them to vote against Clinton, others could interpret the ad as concluding that recognizing homosexual rights was bad policy. The television spot's appearance in the weeks leading up to a presidential election did not, in the judge's eyes, justify restricting freedom of expression. "The First Amendment does not include a proviso stating 'except in elections' and the court refuses to accept an approach to the express advocacy standard that would effectuate such a result," Turk wrote.[8] His ruling was upheld on appeal.

The AFL-CIO and the Business Consortium

With CAN's 1995 victory in the federal district court, the way was cleared for an explosion of issue advocacy. Recognizing that the current system had big loopholes, groups in quick succession announced plans for issue ads. For example, the AFL-CIO indicated it would spend $35 million in 1996 running commercials in the districts of members of Congress who opposed labor objectives. Even though the spots would be broadcast right before the election, mention the names of the Republican representatives, and present unfavorable commentary on their voting records, the AFL-CIO declared these expenditures to be issue advocacy and therefore not subject to federal disclosure rules.[9]

Shortly after labor announced its plans, a consortium of thirty-five business groups, including the U.S. Chamber of Commerce, the National Restaurant Association, and the National Association of Manufacturers, said it would spend $17 million on a pro-business advocacy campaign defending the targeted Republican incumbents. Because these efforts were presented under the guise of public education as opposed to electoral advocacy, they, too, were not subject to federal campaign laws.

Quickly, such groups as the Sierra Club, National Right to Life Committee, Americans for Limited Terms, National Right to Work Committee, American Property Rights Alliance, Small Business Survival Committee, and the National Abortion and Reproductive Rights League announced that they would take to the airwaves as well.[10]

For example, first-term Republican House member Dick Chrysler of Michigan was the object of $2 million worth of advertising in 1996. According to a magazine report, "Sierra Club ads have clobbered Chrysler for voting 'to weaken clean water and air standards.' Citizen Action, a Washington consumer group, accused him (mistakenly, he says) of voting for medicare cuts. The AFL-CIO and the Democratic National Committee (DNC) piled on with their own anti-Chrysler ads."[11] Dozens of other legislators were targeted for similar attacks.

By the time the 1996 election was over, analysts estimated that between $135 and $150 million had been spent by thirty-one different groups on advertisements.[12] Roughly one out of every three dollars expended on commercials in that campaign was devoted to issue ads. Some of them involved only the presidential campaign, but many were run in congressional races across the country. Messages funded by conservative groups attacked Democrats for raising taxes, opposing a balanced budget, or failing to support welfare reform. Liberals, meanwhile, used their spots to blast Republicans for cutting funding for Medicare, education, and environmental programs.

What started as a trickle of issue advocacy now has become a torrent on every conceivable topic. In the last few years, groups interested in health care, tort reform, term limits, a balanced budget, and global warming have blanketed the airwaves with commercials promoting their point of view. Once the exception more than the rule, television spots have become the latest form of political volleyball on controversial issues.[13]

Issue Ads by Political Parties in 1996

Following the path made by outside groups, political parties have discovered issue ads as a legal way to evade campaign spending limits. For example, the Republican National Committee in 1996 aired generic, "cookie-cutter" commercials in New Jersey, Minnesota, Montana, New Hampshire, South Dakota, Rhode Island, and other states complaining that Democratic U.S. Senate candidates were "liberals" who opposed welfare reform and a balanced budget.

Because this and other RNC commercials fell under the category of public education, as opposed to appeals expressly designed to hurt the prospects of a particular candidate, they did not count against the campaign contribution limits on what the committee could give to Republican senatorial candidates.

Each spot ended, not with the tagline "Vote against Jack Reed" (or some other Democrat), which would have made it an election ad in the eyes of the FEC, but rather with these words: "Call liberal Jack Reed. Tell him his record on welfare is just too liberal for you. Tell him to vote for the [Republican] Governor's plan to replace welfare with workfare." By having viewers call the candidate's office about a piece of legislation, such commercials avoided an appeal that would have made them an overt campaign advertisement.[14]

In the 1996 presidential campaign, the Democratic National Committee devoted more than $20 million to educational advertising featuring President Bill Clinton and attacking such "extremist" Republicans as Senator Bob Dole and Speaker Newt Gingrich. Not to be outdone, the RNC ran its own $20 million campaign promoting Dole and attacking Clinton. To make sure that these expenditures did not count against the $12 million limit imposed on each party during the general election for promoting its presidential nominee, both sides labeled these issue advocacy, not election, commercials.

For voters, issue ads are virtually indistinguishable from election spots. In a series of focus groups run during 1996, only 50 percent of participants were able to correctly identify the sponsors of ads in a U.S. Senate race. The reason was clear. Even though issue ads do not say to vote for or against a candidate, they do discuss campaign topics, talk about the contenders and show their pictures, and air right before an election. Since they are interspersed on the air with commercials broadcast by the candidates' official organizations, voters see them as election ads.

About the only real beneficiaries of these spots are the media consultants, who make large commissions from ad buys. Up to 15 percent of the money spent on broadcasting commercials goes to the individuals who produce them. With millions of dollars now devoted to televised appeals, behind-the-scenes operatives have a clear personal stake in perpetuating the current system.

The 1998 Elections

Spending on issue ads rose even more dramatically two years later. According to an Annenberg Public Policy Center study after the 1998 election, somewhere between $275 and $340 million was spent by seventy-seven organizations. This was double the amount of issue advertising in the 1996 elections.[15]

The National Republican Senatorial Committee was one of the largest spenders. Unlike 1996, however, when most money was devoted to independent expenditures, the NRSC shifted in 1998 to funding issue ads by state parties. Overall, more than $9.9 million was transferred from the national body so that local party organizations could broadcast public education advertisements. This was more than six times what the GOP had transferred in 1996.[16]

On the House side, the National Republican Congressional Committee devoted $37 million to Operation Breakout for issue ads. About one-third of these criticized Democrats in connection with Clinton's personal behavior with the former White House intern Monica Lewinsky. Congressional Democrats meanwhile transferred around $9.6 million to state party organizations for issue ads.[17]

Groups from the AFL-CIO and the Business Roundtable to the Sierra Club and the National Right to Life Committee spent millions on public education appeals during the 1998 elections.[18] For example, worried about labor's $35 million expenditure in 1996, thirty-three business organizations formed a group called The Coalition: Americans Working for Real Change, which ran business-oriented issue spots. For its part, labor scaled back its television campaign, on the assumption that midterm election would have low turnout, and instead devoted its cash to get-out-the-vote efforts.

From the Christian Action Network case, therefore, sprang a torrent of commercials that are now about as common as candidate-sponsored advertisements. Rather than relying just on contestants' spending, parties and groups are supplementing official efforts with expenditures that fall outside the system of public disclosure.

Problems of Issue Advocacy

Advertising campaigns focused on particular topics now have become more the norm than the exception. Once only sporadically a part of electioneering, they are commonplace today in closely contested elections. Indeed, interest groups and parties target competitive races for public education advertisements on the assumption that issue-based commercials in these kinds of contests can deliver messages that would be unseemly when put forth by candidates themselves.

This incorporation of issue advocacy into American elections has created a number of difficulties for our political system. Foremost are the problems of secrecy, disclosure, and poor accountability. Issue advocacy takes place outside any required public disclosure of spending or contributors. Direct gifts and campaign contributions to legislators must be revealed, but there are no rules requiring funding of issue advocacy campaigns to be disclosed because the courts say they are not designed to influence the election.

Our current campaign finance system is based on the public's right to know who provides the money and how much is being spent; in the case of presidential contests, it also sets limits on how much each candidate can spend. Without detailed and up-to-date information on campaign finance, voters are in a weaker position to evaluate candidates' credentials and judge who best can represent their views.

Another problem relates to how issue ads have debased the civility and content of campaign discourse. The types of appeals found in these commercials tend to be more negative and less oriented toward specific topics. For example, in 1998, 70 percent of issue ads broadcast within two months of the election were financed by the political parties. For the entire election, two-thirds of the issue ads were sponsored by groups. In comparing spots put on by the parties with candidates' commercials, researchers found that 59.5 percent of issue ads attacked the opposition; this was true of only 23.9 percent of the spots put on by candidates. As this study's director, Kathleen Hall Jamieson, sees it, politicians have worked out a good cop/bad cop routine in which parties attack while candidates advocate.[19]

This calls to mind the 1988 two-track system used by the Bush campaign in the Horton independent expenditure. What started out as a novel electoral strategy a decade ago currently is taken for granted. Issue ads and independent expenditures allow candidates to bypass spending and disclosure laws and also give them more strategic flexibility in determining who delivers hard-hitting messages.

Court rulings that define issue advocacy as distinct from electioneering fail to take into account how new campaign practices and political strategies erase the line between the two. The clear boundary marked out in *Buckley* more than twenty years ago has been obliterated by shifts in technology and tactics. Political opponents and the public alike see advertisements featuring the name and likeness of candidates broadcast in the few months leading up to an election as what, for all practical purposes, they are—campaign appeals. As such, they need to be subject to current rules.

More fundamentally, trends connected with issue advocacy exacerbate problems of equity in American politics. Because of their high cost, television commercials simply are not available to most organized interests as a strategic resource. Only a small percentage of groups are able to afford to employ these new political communications tactics. It generally takes several million dollars of ad buys to get noticed in national politics, a sum that is clearly beyond the means of many citizens' associations, public interest organizations, and insurgent groups.[20]

As the democratic theorist E. E. Schattschneider predicted long ago, this inequity in financial resources has created a political situation where "the heavenly chorus sings with a strong upper-class accent."[21] Money always has been crucial in American politics, but as advocacy comes to require ever more access to financial resources, a relative lack of funds becomes an even more serious barrier to democratic government.

The risk is that our entire system of political debate will become skewed in favor of the well-organized and the well-financed. To the extent that financial resources distinguish serious from less serious players, interests with access to money are able to dominate public deliberation and election campaigns. Established organizations such as business groups, trade associations, and large labor unions are particularly advantaged because of their monetary resources and full-time, professional staffs. Haphazardly funded and staffed grassroots organizations, by contrast, are at a systematic disadvantage in advocacy battles waged through television.

At one level, legal concern over rights of free expression of this area is perfectly understandable. The First Amendment is a pillar of American democracy, and the exercise of these rights is crucial to our system of government. Anything that restricts freedom of speech is potentially damaging to democratic discourse.

But what is often ignored in discussions of money and politics is how our current campaign finance system needs to balance freedom of expression with fairness in political competition. For monied interests from any part of the political spectrum to secretly finance public education ads right before an election eviscerates federal disclosure rules. By the simple act of labeling campaign advertisements as issue advocacy, both outside groups and political parties ensure that they have to disclose nothing about their campaign finances. They are subject to no requirements about naming their contributors or disclosing their spending.

In the long run, this endangers the public's right to know who is behind candidates for office. It exposes contenders to risk from controversial fundraising tactics that backfire. It puts even more limits on the amount of information that is freely available. It complicates the task of reporters whose job it is to follow the money trail. It takes us back to the secrecy and deception of the pre-Watergate system for funding American elections. In the end, it is a system that serves no one's interests well.

CHAPTER 4

Contribution Limits: George Steinbrenner and Simon Fireman

L ATE IN THE nineteenth century, the Republican moneyman Mark Hanna gained fame and political prestige for assessing formal contribution quotas on businesses. Banks were expected to contribute one-quarter of 1 percent of their operating capital to the GOP in order to do business with the government.[1] Other large companies were treated the same way, with each being given a definite expectation as to what its contribution should be. It was old-fashioned fundraising, based on the ability to pay.

Not surprisingly, financial institutions and other large corporations were eager to meet their quotas. National prosperity had increased dramatically in the time following the Civil War, and the new tycoons were more than happy to comply with Hanna's requests. After all, it made good business sense to help politicians in need. His system of quotas made Hanna one of the most successful political fundraisers in the history of the country.

In the years that followed, numerous large contributors gave hundreds of thousands of dollars to particular candidates. One recipient was Warren Harding. After three aspirants deadlocked at the GOP's nominating convention in 1920, his party turned to the senator from Ohio. He was elected as the twenty-ninth president with more than 60 percent of the vote.

Although Harding was personally honest, many in his administration were not, and it is remembered as one of the most corrupt in U.S. history. His secretary of the interior, Albert Fall, was caught up in scandal when it became known that he had secretly leased federal oil reserves (at Teapot Dome, Wyoming) to business friends in return for personal gifts. A number of persons within the administration went to jail and served long sentences on fraud charges.[2]

Similar tales surround Lyndon Johnson. Early in his political career, the congressman was backed by oil interests and was given a broadcasting license to build his personal assets. In his biography of Johnson, Robert Caro documents how large and secret contributions turned him from a dirt-poor politician into a wealthy man.[3]

The General Motors heir Steward Mott was legendary for his support of liberal Democrats. He contributed $200,000 to the antiwar presidential candidate Eugene McCarthy in 1968 and $400,000 to the antiwar nominee George McGovern in 1972. On the right, the Chicago insurance magnate W. Clement Stone delivered nearly $3 million to Richard Nixon in 1968 and $2 million more in 1972. Another conservative activist, Richard Mellon Scaife, donated $1 million to Nixon in 1972.

Overall in 1972, 1,254 individuals donated over $50 million to political candidates, an average of around $40,000 per contributor.[4] Whereas some of them donated to but one candidate, others spread their largesse around to hedge their bets. After all, if the goal was obtaining access, donors did not want to risk backing a loser.

Until the Watergate scandal exploded in the early 1970s, this practice of wealthy men and women contributing large sums to political candidates was quite common. Indeed, it was part of American culture for big money interests (so-called fat cats) to finance individual politicians.

With Watergate, though, things changed radically. Reformers made it illegal for wealthy persons to contribute large amounts of money to a single candidate. New campaign finance rules imposed low limits on the size of specific contributions, as well as on how much contributors could donate to candidates in general. The goal was to eliminate the power of the rich to buy those seeking office and to exercise disproportionate clout with public officials.

These changes wrought a revolution in campaign financing. Candidates were forced to develop new fundraising strategies, and groups and individuals who wanted to influence the political process had to alter their approach. Donors, whether collective or single, had to spread their money over many different contestants and were limited to gifts of $5,000 and $1,000, respectively, to any one candidate in each election stage.

Over two decades, however, major openings developed in the kind and amount of political contributions that were allowed. Large, soft-money donations to political parties have been legalized on grounds of freedom of expression. Issue advocacy and independent expenditures allow wealthy interests to funnel unlimited money into politics in ways that clearly run contrary to what the Watergate reformers had in mind.

Now, the fat cats have returned with a vengeance. Millions can be spent on particular races as long as donors understand the money must be transferred in particular ways, such as through soft-money gifts to parties, expenditures for issue ads, or the creation of or donations to foundations and non-profits interested in the political process.

These and other gaping loopholes point to the clear irrationality of laws governing contributors. Direct campaign contributions to candidates by individuals are limited to $1,000 per election stage, whereas unlimited (and sometimes undisclosed) donations are allowed to political parties. Both individuals and groups can devote any amount they want to independent expenditures or issue advocacy.

This regularly schizophrenia pushes parties and candidates into creative end runs around campaign finance laws, tactics that expose contributors to selective legal enforcement and punishment for white-collar crime. A hallmark of the American justice system is that the law makes a clear distinction between wrongdoing and law-abiding behavior. Unfortunately, campaign finance rules no longer provide that kind of direction. Contributors face wildly different circumstances, depending on how they give money and what jurisdiction they live in. Simply put, the law in this area has become unworkable.

This chapter examines the transformation in campaign finance laws and explains why it is time to rethink the notion of contributor limits. With the rise of unlimited spending in the areas of soft money, independent expenditures, and issue advocacy, it makes little sense to continue to limit the direct contributions of individual donors to $1,000. These developments make a mockery of the legal system and heighten the cynicism of citizens and donors alike about the political process.

The Watergate Scandal

Richard Nixon raised nearly $60 million for his 1972 presidential campaign, giving him more than twice the funds of his Democratic opponent, George McGovern. Using the powers of incumbency, his political operatives were enormously successful in attracting financial support from a variety of wealthy individuals and major business interests. Groups representing the dairy industry, telecommunications, airlines, oil companies, and defense contractors were among Nixon's largest donors, even though it was technically illegal for corporations to make political contributions.

Led by the former secretary of commerce, Maurice Stans, Nixon's fundraisers were so systematic in their efforts that they revived Mark Hanna's old practice of contribution quotas. Large companies were expected to donate at least $100,000, campaign officials made it known, if they wanted to receive favorable treatment from the Nixon White House. As in Hanna's day, corporations eagerly complied with the fundraising requests.

The only problem was that they were breaking the law. Following the election, twenty-one companies were found guilty of making illegal contributions totaling nearly $1 million. Among the corporations prosecuted were Gulf Oil, Braniff Airways, Goodyear, 3M, and American Airlines.[5]

With so much cash flowing into the campaign, money was available for a variety of traditional and not so traditional activities. As in Nixon's first successful run for the presidency in 1968, the biggest expenditures were for television advertising. Befitting the new media era that was emerging, Nixon placed heavy emphasis on direct communication with voters. They were the ultimate goal in the election, and persuading them took highest priority in the campaign.

However, given the large warchest at their disposal, the president's men also turned to more creative enterprises. In order to exert maximum leverage on the electoral process, Nixon sought intelligence on possible opponents, from Ted Kennedy and Edmund Muskie to the ultimate nominee, McGovern. If incriminating information or insights into strategy could be obtained, it could be used to discredit or weaken the opposition.

Hearing rumors about compromising information held at Democratic National Committee headquarters in Washington, top White House officials authorized an illegal break-in at the DNC's offices in the Watergate complex. The goal was to find any information that could be useful to the Nixon re-election effort, such as background material, data on the business dealings of candidates, and personnel files.

This effort, funded by large, secret contributors, typified the mentality of the campaign. His highly successful fundraising allowed Nixon to pursue options that most candidates could not have afforded. In addition to the Watergate break-in, dirty tricks against opponents were planned and executed. Spies were placed in various campaigns. Disruptions of Democratic rallies were encouraged. It was a well-planned, systematic, and highly coordinated operation.

Unfortunately for the Nixon White House, the Watergate burglars were caught red-handed by a late-night security guard. Patrolling the hallways near the Democratic National Committee offices, he noticed tape holding a door unlocked. Investigating further, the officer found the unauthorized men inside DNC headquarters. The guard then radioed the D.C. police, who came and arrested the burglars.

In the ensuing months, Nixon staffers downplayed the break-in and denied any knowledge of it or related activities. The burglars, part of a secret unit called the "plumbers," were operating independently and on their own initiative, according to the White House line. In what was to become one of his most famous remarks, Nixon's press secretary, Ron Ziegler, condemned the break-in as a "third-rate burglary" that had not been authorized by the president.

Slowly, however, the conspiracy of silence that surrounded Nixon's secret campaign activities began to fall apart. An inquisitive judge named John Sirica and two enterprising young reporters at the *Washington Post* named Bob Woodward and Carl Bernstein pushed the investigation. Eventually, the secrets began to emerge.

The break-in was not an isolated action. It was, rather, part of a much larger operation designed to harass Democratic candidates and provide secret intelligence information to the White House for use in the presidential campaign. Not only were the activities massive and fully funded, but they were coordinated by top members of the staff and the president himself.

For months, Nixon continued to deny these facts and condemn the investigation as a witch-hunt. Unknown to investigators, though, the president had a secret taping system in the Oval Office that automatically recorded all conversations. As soon as the system was revealed, tapes were subpoenaed. The Supreme Court ordered the release of the tapes; these clearly demonstrated that the president had been lying when he denied any knowledge of the break-in, the dirty-tricks campaign, and the resulting cover-up of the whole enterprise.

Facing the prospect of impeachment, Nixon resigned in August 1974, humiliated by his efforts to undermine the democratic process. The year of unrelenting press coverage had taken its toll. The president's job approval ratings had plummeted. When the secret tapes confirmed Nixon's participation in the illegal schemes, he was left with the choice of either resigning or being impeached by the House of Representatives and convicted by the Senate.

The scandal would lead to dramatic changes in our system of campaign finance and new efforts to deal with the complex problem of money and politics. What had loomed as a persistent failure on the part of the Congress to deal with fundraising abuses brought on a revolution in finance rules. For the first time in the country's history, legislators systematically addressed the corrupting features of the American money machine.

Post-Watergate Reforms

When the full scope of Nixon's activities became known, both the people and the Washington establishment were outraged. The president's dirty-tricks campaign was the most organized effort to undermine American elections in this century. Featuring break-ins, spying, planting false information, and discrediting the opposition, it was about as fundamental a challenge to representative government as our country had ever witnessed.

Taking advantage of public discontent, politicians embarked on the most massive effort to clean up politics in the history of the United States. Reformers successfully persuaded Congress that a variety of changes should be implemented: contributions should be limited in size and disclosed to the general public, spending should be restricted, presidential campaigns should be publicly financed, and a new federal agency should be created to enforce election laws.

Expenditures should be limited in order to curtail the escalating costs of American campaigns and to place the parties on an equal footing. In preceding presidential elections, Republican nominees typically outspent Democrats by a two-to-one margin. This gave the GOP enormous advantages in the electoral process, among them allowing it to communicate twice as many messages directly to the American people.

Public financing was designed to reduce the power of contributions from private interests. Elections were considered so important as to warrant the spending of tax dollars. A system featuring matching contributions in the nominating process and completely public funding in the general election would help candidates address collective interests unburdened by financial conflicts of interest.

The idea behind the contribution limit was that for the rich to make large (and oftentimes secret) contributions eroded public faith in government by creating the appearance, and sometimes the reality, of corruption. In a system that prided itself on "one person, one vote," big-money gifts also ran smack into the equity principle. How, critics asked, could ordinary women and men trust government officials to do the right thing when individual donors were giving them hundreds of thousands of dollars?

The power of this argument was so compelling to members of Congress that in 1974 they passed a landmark campaign finance bill that limited individuals to contributions of $1,000 per candidate in each election stage. Political action committees affiliated with businesses and labor unions were allowed to give no more than $5,000 per candidate in any one election. The hope was to remove at least the appearance of corruption from the American political system.

The George Steinbrenner Case

Almost immediately after the series of new rules became law, a highly publicized test case came along. Taking advantage of the tough regulations concerning the size of contributions, federal officers indicted George Steinbrenner, the flamboyant owner of the New York Yankees and president of the American Ship Building Company. He was charged with money laundering for purposes of influencing the 1972 election between Nixon and McGovern.

According to the fourteen-count indictment filed against him, Steinbrenner gave bonuses to a number of employees and then ordered them to contribute a total of $100,000 to Nixon's campaign in their own names. They were also instructed to provide gifts to the re-election efforts of two Democratic senators, Daniel Inouye of Hawaii and Vance Hartke of Indiana. In addition, the government accused Steinbrenner of "trying to influence and intimidate employees into lying to a grand jury" about the laundering once it became known in order to minimize his legal exposure.[6]

Prosecutors claimed Steinbrenner's actions were a clear and systematic effort to circumvent the new finance rules limiting contributors to $1,000 gifts. Initially, he pleaded not guilty and tried to contest the charges. However, as part of a plea bargain later in 1974 the Yankee owner pleaded guilty to a felony and a misdemeanor. He admitted to violating the new campaign finance law and attempting to cover up the effort.

After this admission, Steinbrenner was fined $15,000 personally and his company $20,000, but he was spared any jail time. For a felony plea that went to the heart of the new campaign laws, not to mention the attendant perjury charge, the fines were minuscule. The plea bargain indicated that even though new rules were in place enforcement would not be very aggressive.

Reinforcing this message some time later, two days before leaving office in 1989 President Reagan pardoned Steinbrenner for these crimes and restored full citizenship rights to him, including the right to vote.[7] It was an ignoble end to the first major enforcement action against illegal contributions of the post-Watergate era.

Steinbrenner's case was not unusual. His indictment was followed in 1976 by one involving the businessman Armand Hammer. Accused of funneling $54,000 in illegal contributions to Nixon's 1972 campaign, Hammer pleaded guilty; he received no fine and a year's probation. Again, the message was unmistakable. Breaking the law would bring indictment, but the penalty amounted to little more than a slap on the wrist for the rich.

It was not only individuals who faced prosecution under the statutes limiting contributions. A major business, American Airlines, was indicted for wiring money to an agent in Lebanon, supposedly for the purchase of aircraft. Instead, though, the cash was sent back to a U.S. bank, which then made a contribution to Nixon's re-election campaign.[8] Faced with incriminating evidence, the company quietly settled the matter and went on doing business with the federal government.

The Simon Fireman Case

Twenty years later, another investigation arose on the national scene that would further test the law on contribution limits. Simon C. Fireman, a wealthy Massachusetts businessman, was charged by the federal government with violating rules limiting individual campaign gifts to $1,000. He was the founder and chairman of Aqua-Leisure, an international distributor of swimming goggles, flippers, inflatable pool toys, and physical fitness equipment. Well connected in national political circles, Fireman had served as director of the Export-Import Bank under Reagan, had been Bush's national vice chairman for finance in 1992, and was national vice chairman of finance for Robert Dole's presidential campaign in 1996.[9]

During an analysis of campaign contributions to Dole's election effort, reporters for the *Kansas City Star* found several unusual patterns. Between February and September 1995 at least forty workers at Aqua-Leisure had made identical contributions of $1,000 to Dole's campaign. Twelve gifts from Aqua-Leisure employees all arrived on February 28, 1995. And it was not only top managers and salesmen who made contributions; individuals who worked for the company as secretaries, bookkeepers, and warehouse managers gave $1,000 donations to Dole. Copies of bank records revealed that "large amounts of cash flowed into contributor's bank accounts just before they donated" the money.[10]

Interviewed on national television, the candidate immediately called for an official investigation. Appearing on the CBS news show *Face the Nation,* Dole said, "It's an allegation that's been made and ought to be checked. If somebody did [make illegal donations], they're in deep trouble . . . they are going to have to suffer the consequences."[11]

According to news accounts, Fireman's executive assistant, Carol Nichols, approached company employees with cash and asked them to make contributions to Dole. Several workers interviewed on the record denied being pressured to make a donation. Others claimed they had not been reimbursed by the company. Yet several employees contacted off the record contradicted these accounts and claimed workers at Aqua-Leisure were given "stacks of $100 bills and told to return with checks made out to 'Dole for President.' "[12]

Both the Federal Election Commission and the Department of Justice ordered investigations. Not only was it illegal to funnel money through others and to exceed the $1,000 individual contribution limit, but any one person was prohibited from donating more than $25,000 to a candidate in any calendar year.

By July 1996 a plea bargain was reached between Fireman and the U.S. attorney. He pleaded guilty to evading the $1,000 contributor limit by funneling around $120,000 in cash to employees so that they could donate the money to various campaign organizations: $69,000 to Dole, $21,000 to Bush in 1992, $6,000 to Representative Joseph Kennedy, and $24,000 to the Republican National Committee. These amounts were roughly comparable to the $100,000 in illegal contributions made by George Steinbrenner in the 1970s. The Federal Election Commission later dropped its own investigation into the matter.

According to court filings, officials of Aqua-Leisure employed wire transfers from a Hong Kong company named Rickwood Limited and a secret trust established at a bank in the United States to send thousands of dollars into the secret U.S. account, which then could be distributed as cash in small amounts. After admitting his guilt, Fireman was fined $1 million, sentenced to six months of home confinement, and given two years of probation. His Aqua-Leisure company was fined $5 million and placed on probation for four years.[13]

During the home confinement, Fireman had to wear an electronic monitor, not conduct business, do no entertaining, and use only a phone that was monitored and could be recorded, similar to those used by inmates at a county jail.[14] Visitors were permitted three times a week for no more than an hour at a time. Use of on-line computers was forbidden.

This was the toughest sentence yet imposed in a contributor-limit case. To put it in context, when Steinbrenner pleaded guilty in 1974 to making $100,000 in illegal contributions and pressuring employees to cover up the crimes, his total fine was $35,000 and he received no prison sentence or home confinement. Armand Hammer was neither fined nor jailed. In fact, the highest penalty to date for funneling illegal contributions through company employees had been the $600,000 assessed against Hyundai Motor America for donations to Representative Jay Kim of California.

In 1995, Dominic Saraceno, the treasurer of Alexander Haig's 1988 presidential campaign, was sentenced to four months of home confinement, given two years of probation, and fined $20,000 after he pleaded guilty to charges of lying to the Federal Election Commission when he denied knowing the Haig committee had been given illegal contributions of his. Saraceno had distributed $1,000 apiece to forty-six employees to use however they wanted. Eight of them gave money to Haig's presidential effort, which helped the aspirant qualify for federal matching funds. In the court filing, Saraceno "admitted that he had lied when he told the Federal Election Commission that he was not aware of any improper contributions to the Haig campaign."[15] Donald Cooke Jr., a fellow businessman, was fined $500 after pleading guilty "to lying when he said he had not reimbursed his employees for their [Haig] contributions . . .

[and] when he denied that Saraceno had asked him to say that."[16]

To cite one last example, in 1999 the Democratic fundraiser Howard Glicken was fined $40,000 by the Federal Election Commission, and received a fine of $80,000 plus 18 months of probation and 500 hours of community service from a U.S. district court, for fundraising violations. In 1993, Glicken had raised money for the Democratic Senatorial Campaign Committee from a foreign national named Thomas Kramer; he encouraged the donor to have someone else sign the check so as to conceal the illegal contribution. Kramer eventually was fined $323,000 for making unlawful contributions totaling $418,600 in 1993 and 1994 to a variety of political candidates.[17]

When he was asked why Simon Fireman's 1996 penalty was so severe, U.S. Attorney Donald Stern pointed to "the elaborate lengths to which Mr. Fireman had gone to keep his scheme from being traced, steps that included wiring from Hong Kong the money that was to be distributed in cash to participating employees."[18]

Thomas Dwyer, a lawyer for Fireman, proposed another explanation in a statement released the day of sentencing, two weeks before the election: "It is our feeling that Mr. Fireman was subjected to a penalty which resulted from the government's necessity to get a big fine in an election year. . . . If this were not a political season, we believe the case would have been resolved for substantially less money."[19]

Although there was no indication that the Dole campaign or any of the other organizations involved were aware of the money laundering, Bill Clinton's spokesman Joe Lockhart immediately put the case into the middle of the presidential contest by strongly criticizing the Republican candidate: "It's now clear that there was criminal activity within the Dole campaign. Bob Dole needs to explain his relationship with Mr. Fireman [and] what role, if any, anyone in his campaign had in this illegal operation."[20]

Aware of their own side's political vulnerability on campaign fundraising (which was to explode in the closing days of the race), Clinton staffers sought to tie Dole to Fireman in order to make it look like the Republican nominee had been complicit in illegal fundraising. During a Dole campaign trip through the Northeast, for example, when the Kansan criticized Clinton for illegally raising funds from foreign contributors, Lockhart counterpunched: "Bob Dole is in New England. Maybe while he's there talking about campaign finance, he can take time to visit his old friend Simon Fireman, if the parole officer will let him."[21]

It was a "spin" tactic the Clinton damage-control machine would employ again and again against political foes.[22] Whether the scandal be Whitewater, campaign finance, or impeachment, Clinton believed the best defense was a good offense against opponents. If the people doubt the messenger, they are unlikely to believe the message. Recognizing that his own fundraising abuses would come to light at some point, the president's public relations managers sought to inoculate their boss against public perceptions that he had broken the law in his own presidential campaign. After all, if everybody was doing it, the voters could not impose any political penalty.

The Current Irrationality in Contributor Limits

The two decades between the Steinbrenner and Fireman cases (and others less notorious) have seen the unraveling of the system intended to regulate campaign contributions. There was a logic to the reforms of the 1970s. It was important to restore equity to electoral competition, so candidates were publicly financed and each party was given the same amount for electioneering. Concerns about the corrupting power of big money led to low contributor limits and restrictions on the overall amount individuals could expend in any single year. Tough disclosure rules were put in place so that the public could see who was financing American campaigns. A strong agency, the Federal Election Commission, was created to enforce the law.

For a time, these measures appeared to work. Facing a disillusioned, cynical public following the Watergate scandal and Nixon's resignation, candidates ran on themes of trust and were cautious about how they raised and spent money. Dirty tricks were out and fair electoral competition was in. It was important to play by commonly accepted rules and to be seen as fair-minded by the people.

Over the course of the past twenty years, however, several trends have destroyed the original logic behind campaign finance reform. A series of court cases designed to resolve ambiguities in the congressional legislation and the Supreme Court's subsequent decision in *Buckley v. Valeo* opened gaping holes in legal enforcement. Emboldened by these rulings, both candidates and interest groups have become more aggressive at exploiting inconsistencies in the law.

Between the sharp increase in the number of campaign finance loopholes and changing patterns of candidate and interest group behavior, there is now a very different political situation in regard to money. In fact, we have reached a point where current rules governing campaign finance are irrational at their core. Behavior that is condemned and forbidden in one form is tolerated and practiced in another. Nothing illustrates this problem more than the law on contribution limits.

Donors can give hundreds of thousands of dollars in soft money to political parties, which funds can then be used to buy ads and otherwise support the election of specific candidates. In 1996, for example, the National Republican Senatorial Committee, chaired by Senator Alfonse D'Amato of New York, routinely used soft-money contributions to broadcast ads in individual Senate races that extolled or criticized specific candidates. The ads were virtually identical to commercials broadcast by the Republican nominees themselves, in some cases even being produced by the same media consultants.

In the 1996 presidential campaign, Bob Dole was supported by ads paid for by the Republican National Committee outside election spending limits, ads that relied on the same footage and arguments as spots financed by his own campaign. The same held true for Bill Clinton and the Democrats. Advertising consultants slid effortlessly between working on commercials for candidates and on independent commercials broadcast by the Democratic National Committee.

Current rules allow unlimited contributions to fund independent expenditures like Bush's "Weekend Passes" ad and issue advocacy campaigns like that run by the Christian Action

Network. For example, if a group wanted to spend millions proclaiming the virtues of Elizabeth Dole or Al Gore, the expenditure would be perfectly legal so long as the maze of rules laid down in court cases was respected. Independent expenditures cannot be overtly coordinated with the candidate's organization, and issue ads cannot expressly urge voting for or against a specific person.

But in spite of rules that tolerate unrestricted spending in these areas, direct gifts to a candidate for federal office remain limited to $1,000, with total yearly donations limited to $25,000. Even though inflation has eroded the value of these sums over the past two decades, the limits have not been raised since 1974, have not been indexed to inflation, and have not been altered in light of new political circumstances. The resultant legal situation offers little coherence or fairness.

Not surprisingly, courts are starting to reconsider the constitutionality of the rules in this domain. For example, following a challenge to a 1994 Missouri law restricting contributors to $1,000 for an entire election, the United States Court of Appeals for the Eighth Circuit in St. Louis struck down the statute on November 30, 1998. According to the judges, the limits were "so small that they run afoul of the Constitution by unnecessarily restricting protected First Amendment freedoms."[23]

The judges in this case, *Nixon v. Shrink Missouri Government PAC,* found (using a campaign cost-of-living formula) that the inflation-adjusted value of the $1,000 contributor limit of 1974 would be $2,500 in 1998 dollars. An appeal is pending before the U.S. Supreme Court as to whether *Buckley*-imposed contributor limits are still constitutional. Lower courts have struck down limits of $100 per election in the District of Columbia and similarly low restrictions in Alaska, California, and Oregon on the grounds that they restrict freedom of speech.[24]

Since soft-money contributions, independent expenditures, and donations for issue ads fund virtually the same kinds of activities as do direct contributions to candidates, it makes little sense to fine someone millions of dollars for actions that are engaged in by dozens of individuals, corporations, and unions.

Indeed, vague and inconsistent rules lead to selective enforcement and unfair prosecution. Contributors can no longer be sure that their gifts will not expose them to being charged with white-collar crimes. Depending on what kind of donation they make, they are subject to wildly varying laws. This, in turn, breeds cynicism among all involved.

In recent years, soft-money contributions have been one of the fastest growing areas in campaign finance. Once an unknown part of elections, they now play a major role. For example, in 1996 the Amway executive Richard DeVos and his wife contributed $1 million to the Republican National Committee; the tobacco company Philip Morris gave the RNC over $760,000 in 1997; and in the same year, the actor and comedian Robin Williams gave $100,000 to the Democratic National Committee.[25]

Such contributions, large though they may seem, are merely the tip of the iceberg. Dozens of leading corporations and wealthy individuals have donated hundreds of thousands of dollars to the two party organizations. Once a rarity, such gifts now occur with surprising frequency.

In earlier days, when the distinctions between the kinds of

financial contributions were more substantial, the rules governing limited hard-money and unlimited soft-money donations were not as problematic. There were sharp differences in how the two kinds of money could be spent and a clear idea of how cash would affect the election process.[26]

Today, however, the differences across types of contributions have become clouded, and there are few ways to distinguish between what can be done with soft- versus hard-money gifts. For someone who wants to play by the rules, it is virtually impossible to justify current distinctions in campaign finance law. Soft money can be used to support candidates' activities, television commercials, and public opinion surveys. So can hard money, independent expenditures, and funds nominally devoted to issue advocacy.

It makes no sense to have such a system of elections. Donors need clearer guidelines in order to avoid running afoul of the law. Rules must be precise enough that reasonable citizens can distinguish between actions that are lawful and those that are not. Ironically, penalties and fines for violating campaign finance rules have risen at exactly the time when the clarity of those rules has fallen off dramatically. It is a legal situation that is dangerous for all.

CHAPTER 5

Foreign Nationals and the Democratic National Committee

I N 1995, BILL CLINTON was worried about the upcoming presidential election. Democrats had lost badly in the 1994 midterm contest. Republicans had seized control of both the House and Senate for the first time in forty years. Not only was the GOP well positioned for 1996, but it was also developing a major fundraising advantage over the Democrats. Pundits openly questioned whether Clinton was even relevant to policy debates anymore. His defeat for a second term seemed inevitable, given his party's debacle in its push for health care reform and in the midterm voting.

Following the Democrats' poor performance in those elections, Clinton had fired the team of consultants that had led him to victory in 1992. The strategist James Carville, the pollster Stanley Greenberg, and the media advisor Mandy Grunwald were all dumped. None had adequately foreseen the growing Republican electoral threat.

In their place came an advisor from Clinton's Arkansas days. Dick Morris was an odd duck in many respects. Although political strategists usually did not cross party lines, he had worked for candidates of both parties. Not only was Morris close to Clinton, but he maintained good ties with Senator Trent Lott, leader of the Republican majority in the Senate.

Morris also had a bond with the president that none of the Washington consultants could match. When Clinton had lost a campaign to be re-elected governor of Arkansas, he had turned to Morris to salvage his failing political career. Working closely with Bill and Hillary Clinton, the advisor had reversed the governor's fortunes and helped position him as a centrist, not a liberal, Democrat.[1]

Now Morris made the following recommendation. In order to win the 1996 presidential campaign, Clinton would have to run early television ads extolling his record. The Republicans in charge of Congress had developed a bold new agenda known as the Contract with America. It laid out an ambitious legislative package designed to downsize the federal government, create an "opportunity society," and cut taxes, among other objectives.

Such zealotry was bound to provoke a backlash among sectors of society hurt by massive change. The goals of the early advertising barrage would be to set up Democrats as the bulwark against GOP extremism; develop an alternative agenda of protecting Medicare, education, and the environment; and put the likely Republican presidential nominee, Senator Bob Dole, on the defensive from the very start because of his ties to Newt Gingrich, the unpopular Speaker of the House.[2]

There was only one problem with Morris's plan. It would cost a lot of money, so much as to endanger the president's ability to stay within the election's official spending limits. Each nominee for the White House was required to work with a budget of $65 to $70 million. As various courts had ruled since 1992, extra money could be spent through independent groups and issue ads. But the fundraising drive would have to go into high gear, and soon. Bill Clinton would need more money than had ever been raised in a presidential campaign.

Typically, candidates did not like to spend their scarce dollars on early advertising. Indeed, almost all of the president's Washington advisors spoke out against Morris's plan. Going on television eighteen months before the voting was ludicrous, they argued, because the electorate was not paying attention that far in advance. It was much wiser to save money for the very end of the campaign, when undecided voters did tune in and the election might hang in the balance.

These advisors conceded that some money could be waived from the overall spending cap by using issue ads financed through the Democratic National Committee that would not count against Clinton's general election limit. Court rulings on independent expenditures and issue advocacy made it obvious that cash could be funneled to election ads that would make the president's case.

But the gist of Morris's recommendation was clear to all involved. This would not be a normal campaign. Clinton would need a lot of cash and he would need it up front. The White House would have to get serious to the point of obsession about fundraising. It would have to engage the efforts of everyone— the president and first lady, the vice president, the various staffs. No one would be spared from the fixation on bringing in dollars.

Where would Democrats get the kind of money that was envisioned? They no longer controlled Congress, so it would not be easy to raise funds from interest groups that wanted access to the legislative process. Concomitantly, since they no longer held any committee chairmanships, they could not offer friendly amendments to corporations and other wealthy interests.

Instead, a new strategy was devised. Democrats would develop a creative plan to expand the pool of donors. New groups of constituents who previously had not received much attention would be mobilized, among them Asian Americans and foreign companies with U.S. subsidiaries. Their resources would fund the Clinton re-election effort.

Over the course of ten months, the president attended 237 fundraisers and garnered a total of $119.2 million. This was more than twice the number of such events President Bush had organized in 1992.[3] Clinton would succeed in his fundraising efforts and win re-election over Dole. But in the process he would become engulfed in a scandal that left a bad feeling in the stomachs of all of the political leaders involved. The strategy of raising money early would come back to haunt him.

The Arkansas Connection

In order to implement his fundraising plan, Clinton turned to some old friends from his home state. James Riady owned the Worthen Bank in Little Rock. This small bank did business with the Rose Law Firm, the state's premier legal enterprise. As part of his banking business, Riady had become friends with then Governor Clinton and Hillary Clinton, a partner at Rose.

The Worthen Bank was part of a worldwide business empire called the Lippo Group. The organization specialized in banks, real estate, and energy, among other things. It was controlled by Riady's father, Mochtar Riady, an Indonesian businessman.

Among the Lippo Group's many executives in the United States was John Huang. After his birth in China in 1945, Huang's family had fled to Taiwan in 1949 when the Communists took over the mainland. (His father was a major general in the Chinese Nationalist army.) Huang graduated from Tatung Institute of Technology in 1967 and served as a second lieutenant in the Taiwanese air force. He moved to America in 1969 and earned a master's degree in business from the University of Connecticut.[4] Huang became a naturalized U.S. citizen in 1976.

Starting as a trainee at the American Security Bank in Washington, D.C., Huang eventually rose to assistant vice president. In 1985, he was hired as executive vice president of Lippo's world banking division in Hong Kong. A year later, he was promoted to president and chief operating officer of the Lippo Bank of Los Angeles, which was owned by James Riady.

Huang was a man on a mission: he wanted to boost the political influence of Asian Americans. Living in Los Angeles, he could see that they were rising in local influence but were not being taken very seriously in national politics. Speaking at a meeting organized by Chinese Americans United for Self-Empowerment, he urged members to become engaged in the political process. "Don't just make money," he said. "Get involved. This is your country."[5]

In the 1992 presidential contest, Huang organized a notably successful fundraiser for Clinton in California that brought in a quarter of a million dollars from Asian Americans in the Los Angeles area. It marked the first time they had played so active a part in presidential politics. Still, despite these efforts, Clinton lost the Asian-American vote to George Bush by 55 to 31 percent.[6]

In 1994, after receiving an $879,000 bonus, Huang left the Lippo Group for a top position in Clinton's Department of Commerce. He was the administration's highest-ranking Asian American. At Commerce, Huang served as deputy assistant secretary for international economic policy. The job gave him "access to embassy cables, intelligence reports and classified information that is used to develop U.S. trade policy. This includes the government's positions in active negotiations, discussions about trade sanctions and the activities of foreign governments and foreign competitors."[7] On a number of occasions, Huang and James Riady had private meetings with the president at the executive mansion. Huang himself visited the White House fifty-two separate times.

The 1996 Presidential Campaign

In December 1995 Huang moved to a fundraising position with the Democratic National Committee. According to DNC records described in the "National Asian Pacific American Campaign Plan," the party hoped to raise $7 million from Asian Americans.[8] Even though they made up only about 1 percent of the national electorate, this effort was part of the general move to mobilize new groups as sources of funds and bring them into the political process.

Soon after Huang's arrival, extraordinary contributions started to come in. A South Korean corporation, Cheong Am America, Inc., donated $250,000. An event at a Buddhist temple garnered $140,000. An Indonesian couple gave $425,000 to the DNC.

A July 1996 fundraiser in Los Angeles earned Clinton half a million dollars. A grateful president publicly acknowledged his DNC aide. "I'd like to thank my longtime friend John Huang for being so effective," Clinton said. "Frankly, he's been so effective I was amazed you [the donors] were all cheering for him tonight."[9] In a short time, and without any substantial experience in political fundraising, Huang had brought in several million dollars.

But reporters were starting to learn troubling information. The South Korean corporation that had donated the quarter million dollars had no U.S. subsidiary and did no business in America. This made the gift illegal. According to federal law, foreign citizens or foreign companies are forbidden to donate money to a U.S. candidate or political party. American subsidiaries of overseas corporations could contribute, as long as the money was made from U.S. domestic operations. Foreigners living legally in the United States were free to make donations, too, provided that they maintained an American residence, the money was theirs, and it had not come from overseas.

This last rule was a problem for the Indonesian couple, Arief and Soraya Wiriadinata. After being asked by Huang, they gave the DNC $425,000. The contribution appeared suspicious because the man was a landscape architect who lived in a modest townhouse in Virginia. His wife, however, was the daughter of a wealthy Indonesian businessman, Nashim Ning, who owned part of the Lippo Group.[10] They made their donation after they had returned to live in Jakarta.

The meeting at the Buddhist temple was also problematic. Nuns who had taken a vow of poverty told of being handed thousands of dollars in cash and then being asked by superiors to make a contribution in their own name to the Democrats. Not only did this raise questions politically, smacking as it did of illicit fundraising, but it was a clear violation of federal law. Women and men were allowed to contribute money only if it was their own; cash given to them by someone else could not be donated to a political campaign. Twenty years of prosecutions of such men as Steinbrenner and Fireman had firmly established at least that principle.

As news of the widespread campaign finance violations started to trickle out a few weeks before the general election— Democrats were required to file pre-election fundraising reports—Bob Dole was very critical. "We cannot allow the political influence of any American to be outweighed by foreign money," the Republican nominee complained.[11] What Clinton was doing was just not right, he argued. Federal laws clearly prohibited gifts of the sort that had been uncovered.

Representatives of the Democrats accused the GOP of hypocrisy. Appearing on the CBS interview show *Face the Nation,* the DNC's national chairman, Senator Christopher Dodd of Connecticut, noted that these sorts of fundraising practices were things "that both houses do." He went on to argue that "we need to clean this up. We just wish the Republican National Committee would have taken similar steps. . . . I don't hear a similar complaint . . . when the Dole campaign gets $400,000 from the Brown and Williamson Tobacco Co. of London."[12]

Dodd was being disingenuous. Brown and Williamson was an international company with a big American subsidiary. Campaign gifts from that corporation were clearly, unambiguously legal. However, the senator made it sound as if Republicans were raising money illegally from abroad by noting the London headquarters of Brown and Williamson. Leon Panetta, the White House chief of staff, was more blunt. He accused Republicans of having taken "$2.4 million, $2.5 million themselves from subsidiaries of foreign corporations." The subtext was clear. Democrats should not be penalized for doing what all parties do. Yet again, the rhetoric was designed to obfuscate the truth. It was not illegal to raise money from American subsidiaries of foreign corporations. The law on this point was well known.

Seeking to inoculate Clinton from any further political damage, Panetta then noted that Dole's finance vice chairman, Simon Fireman, was "going to be sentenced this week to about six months in jail" for campaign finance violations.[13] His sentencing had been rushed through in record time, not at all the usual practice in campaign fundraising cases, which generally dragged on for years in the courts. It was, though, the one contribution case where Democrats knew Dole was vulnerable.

To make the point even more clearly, the Clinton forces started airing television ads accusing Dole of "desperate attacks" on the campaign finance front. Republicans, the spot proclaimed, were guilty of the same practices as Democrats. The

GOP was raising money from overseas interests, such as "foreign oil, foreign tobacco, [and] foreign drug companies."[14] Although the charge was true, the ad failed to mention that such gifts were not illegal; each of these foreign businesses had American subsidiaries that were making the campaign contributions to the Republican candidate.

Despite these public counterattacks, still other problems emerged for Democrats. Yogesh Gandhi, the great-grandnephew of Mahatma Gandhi, contributed $325,000 to the DNC following a solicitation from Huang. According to California records, however, he was $10,000 in arrears on his taxes, had failed to pay traffic fines, owed money to friends, and was the subject of at least two legal judgments for unpaid bills.[15] In an August court proceeding, Gandhi, aged forty-seven, claimed that all his income came from a family trust located in India. According to U.S. fundraising laws, his gift was illegal.

In the end, none of these campaign finance controversies harmed President Clinton, although they did hold down Democratic margins and keep Republicans in majority control of the House and Senate. He coasted to victory over Dole and raised his share of the Asian-American vote from 31 percent in 1992 to 43 percent in 1996. Dole, though, still beat him by garnering the support of 48 percent of this group of voters.[16]

By accusing Republicans of engaging in the same nefarious fundraising practices as Democrats did, Clinton neutralized a problem that could have exploded in his face. The only remaining threat was a congressional investigation. After raising $150 million more than the president's party, the Republicans had retained control of the House and Senate. Congressional members of the GOP were incensed because they felt the president had gained an unfair advantage over their party through running early ads funded by illegal gifts. They resolved not to take this outrage lying down.

The Post-Election Investigation

After the voting, the GOP quickly moved toward a full-scale inquiry. In its eyes, what Democrats had done during this election was not just more of the same old thing. The DNC had suspended any background checks on party donors, which previously had helped ensure that money was coming from legitimate sources, and subsequently had raised millions from questionable foreign sources. What had been promised in exchange was an open question, although rumors abounded in Washington of policy reviews and reassessments. In the end, the DNC returned $1.6 of the $3.4 million that John Huang had raised.

As more information came to light about the fundraiser's activities, telephone logs and appointment books revealed that he had devoted most of his time at the Commerce Department to matters involving economic relations with Indonesia, China, and other Asian nations where the Lippo Group did business. Among undertakings in which Huang had been engaged were "meetings to develop commercial strategy between the United States and the Pacific Rim, to organize the annual Asian Pacific Economic Conference, to plan former Commerce Secretary Ronald H. Brown's 1994 trade mission to China and to consult with officials of the U.S. Trade Representative's office." Over thirteen months, Huang had obtained at least thirty-five briefings on U.S. foreign intelligence, especially in matters dealing with American economic policy toward China.[17]

For a midlevel bureaucrat, John Huang had remarkably easy access to the White House. Videotapes of coffees at the executive mansion show him as a frequent guest. He lunched and talked with Webster Hubbell, the former associate attorney general who had been forced to resign over financial irregularities. Hubbell had been a consultant with the Lippo Group before he was imprisoned for two years. Huang also had regular conversations with Mark Middleton, the White House liaison to the business community. President Clinton described Huang as his "good friend."

It was the Chinese connection, though, that especially worried congressional Republicans. During one of Huang's White House meetings with Clinton, James Riady had urged the president "to intensify [his] efforts in China."[18] In particular, Riady was eager for the president "to separate China's trading privileges from human rights concerns." It was time for closer economic ties, he thought.

Others were working toward the same end. After contributing $639,000 to Clinton's legal defense fund, the Arkansas restaurant owner Charlie Yah Lin Trie, an old friend of the president's, was appointed to a commission exploring U.S.-Asian trade. He later arranged for a weapons dealer from China named Wang Jun to meet President Clinton at a private White House coffee.[19]

All of this greatly disturbed Senator Fred Thompson. The Tennessee Republican headed the Senate Committee on Governmental Affairs, which was investigating campaign finance irregularities. Along with other committee members, he had received briefings from the FBI claiming the Chinese government had a systematic plan to influence the 1996 elections. An expert who studied international businesses testified that Lippo had "shifted its strategic center from Indonesia to China." Much of its current activity involved joint ventures with China Resources, a company owned by the Chinese government.[20] According to the expert, Beijing employed that company "as an agent of espionage—economic, military and political."

During his seventeen months at the Commerce Department, Huang made more than four hundred phone calls to the Lippo Group and also used a private office rented by an Arkansas company with ties to Lippo.[21] At one point, he wrote a memo asking Lippo to wire money from Indonesia so he could make a $50,000 contribution to the Democratic party. This provided the most-direct evidence that Huang had funneled illegal money from abroad into the American campaign.

Proving the policy connection to China, though, was far more difficult, and the committee's final report was inconclusive. Unlike other countries, China would not make available to American investigators any banking or financial records. Although the committee produced circumstantial evidence linking Huang and Lippo to the Chinese government, it proved nearly impossible to substantiate a direct connection.[22] Still, the impression left by the investigation was not favorable. As Senator Joseph Lieberman, a Democrat, put it, "[I]f you're soliciting, there are going to be people who are prepared to buy, and some of them are not going to have good motives."[23]

The Cost to Clinton and the Country

By the time the campaign ended, Bill Clinton had attended more than twice as many fundraising events as George Bush had done in 1992. Oftentimes, Clinton would schedule two major appearances in the same hotel an hour apart. As one crowd departed, the next would arrive. Senator Lieberman compared it to "a doctor seeing patients in different waiting rooms." Typical weeks showed fundraising coffees and dinners five or six days out of seven. In March, Clinton organized twenty-two such events; in June, there were thirty; in October, there were twenty-four.[24]

To accommodate such a frenetic money-raising schedule, White House staffers were forced to cancel official presidential meetings. For example, consultations with the Council of Economic Advisers were dropped for long stretches at a time. Briefings by the chief of staff and the national security advisor often gave way to breakfast fundraisers and coffees. Clinton's aides could see the personal drain on the president. One anonymous official observed, "[H]e lost . . . all his down time. He started getting up earlier and going to bed later. All of his rest was gone." Campaign advisors worried about fatigue and its effect on the president's judgment. Dick Morris, the architect of Clinton's successful 1996 strategy, testified under oath about the president's complaints. "He would say, 'I haven't slept in three days; every time I turn around they want me to be at a fund-raiser. . . . I cannot think, I can't do anything.' "[25]

The change in Clinton's attitude toward raising money had

come following the 1994 elections, when Democrats had been drubbed and lost control of Congress. Before that time, officials at the Democratic National Committee described fundraising as "a low priority" and something that made them "very, very frustrated." After the November losses, though, everything changed. Truman Arnold, an oil businessman and longtime Clinton fan, was brought into the DNC. His mandate was to raise $42 million in unrestricted, soft-money contributions. The official Clinton-Gore campaign set its own goal as $25 million. Overall, the DNC concluded, it needed $130 million to be competitive in 1996.[26]

In order to bring in so much money, the party had to devise creative ways to attract donors. All modern presidents have played to contributors who, in return for time with the chief executive, were willing to make a substantial financial gift. But Clinton, Gore, and the DNC took such activities to new levels. Among the key attractions were "state dinner invitations, seats aboard Air Force One, tickets to the White House movie theater, and golf or jogging outings with Clinton."[27] Large contributors even got to sleep overnight in the Lincoln Bedroom. The fundraising operation was systematic, calculated, and ruthlessly efficient.

Occasionally, the strain would show. At one event, the president was so tired that he gave the wrong speech, one on education rather than crime. No doubt the law enforcement people standing behind him were perplexed. At other times he appeared to be going through the motions with donors, to the disappointment of those giving large sums of money. With such a frenetic schedule, it was hard for him to stay on top of the job day after day.

It was not just Clinton who was affected by the exposure of the fundraising plan. By the end of the congressional investigation, the DNC had been forced to return more than $3 million overall in 1997 and 1998. More than a dozen individuals were indicted for illegal fundraising, and a number were convicted.[28] John Huang himself was given immunity by Kenneth Starr, the independent counsel, in return for testimony alleging that Clinton's friend Webster Hubbell "performed little or no work" in exchange for a $100,000 consulting contract from James Riady.[29] Hubbell was a key figure in Starr's investigation into the Whitewater land transactions involving the Clintons and their associates, and the independent counsel hoped he would turn against the president.

The animosity generated among Republicans by the fundraising scandal soon found a new outlet. In the midst of the 1996 campaign, Clinton had carried on a sexual relationship with a young White House intern named Monica Lewinsky. The affair created a crisis. Throughout most of 1998 and into early 1999, the nation was subjected to the unprecedented scandal of a president being accused of committing perjury and obstructing justice, among other things, in an effort to cover up a sexual liaison.

Feeling betrayed by what they saw as Clinton's dishonesty on campaign fundraising, House Republicans pushed for impeachment on issues related to the sex scandal. Many GOP leaders were of the view that the president's behavior in things such as Whitewater and the financing of the 1996 campaign had crossed the line into impropriety. The Lewinsky matter, however, marked the first time they could prove Clinton had lied. Although the president survived politically, he paid a high price in lost personal credibility with members of Congress. Republican legislators no longer trusted him.

As the House debated impeachment of the president, the country was significantly divided. Some felt that the president was being railroaded over a sex scandal and that right-wing groups were behind the extraordinary investigations to which Clinton had been and was being subjected. Others blamed the president and could not understand how the opinion polls indicated that two-thirds of Americans believed he was doing a good job. It was one of the most polarizing episodes of the twentieth century in the United States.[30]

In the end, the House impeached the president on what was nearly a straight party-line vote. However, Clinton survived the Senate trial. Fifty senators voted to remove him from office on grounds of having obstructed justice, well short of the sixty-seven needed to end his presidency.

Yet hard feelings lingered between the two parties. Republicans believed that Clinton had lied to them time and time again. He had run in 1992 as a New Democrat, but then proposed a massive reform of health care, with a major role for government. The president had initiated serious conversation with Republicans about entitlement reform in 1995, but no sooner had they proposed specific changes than he devoted his re-election campaign to complaining about Republican plans to cut Medicare.

In their view, the campaign finance illegalities were part of a much larger pattern.

Unresolved Questions about China

When the fundraising investigation had concluded, the most tantalizing subject remained the China connection. Was money from the People's Republic given in exchange for access to sensitive military technology, as many House Republicans believed? According to a seven-hundred-page report, issued by a special bipartisan House panel led by Representative Christopher Cox, a California Republican, the answer was yes. China had gone to unusual lengths in its search for new technology.

Over the course of six months the committee had held thirty-three closed hearings and heard from a number of military, satellite, and intelligence experts. The nine Republican and Democratic members were disturbed at some of what they found.

Although a substantial part of the specific contents of the report was classified as secret, news stories indicated that China had been trying to steal sensitive U.S. military and satellite technology for more than two decades. The effort had not targeted just the Clinton White House, but rather involved administrations of both parties, stretching back to that of Ronald Reagan.

However, one aspect of the operation was specific to Clinton's presidency. His Commerce Department was accused of failing to adequately monitor the Loral Corporation and Hughes Electronics when they delivered missile technology to

China. Loral's chairman, Bernard Schwartz, long had given large contributions to Democratic candidates. Indeed, in 1996, he had been one of the DNC's largest soft-money donors.

Although the report did not systematically examine the matter of campaign donations from China, the committee did explore the actions of a Chinese aerospace official named Liu Chao-ying. According to Senator Thompson's Governmental Affairs Committee, Mrs. Liu had been involved in funneling money from China to the DNC while with her father, a general in the Chinese military, was trying to gain access to new satellite technology.[31] The tie was purely circumstantial, but partisans felt it might be significant.

One thing was clear. After a Chinese rocket failed in launching a U.S. satellite, Loral had sent China the results of a detailed assessment of the accident. House Speaker Newt Gingrich immediately criticized Clinton. Commenting on the close ties between the president and Loral, Gingrich said the China deal was "the closest thing to an impeachable offense."[32]

The problem was that information on commercial rocket launches was similar to that involved in military rocketry. The fear was not only that China was using this new data for its own military advantage, but that it had sold equipment featuring the sensitive material to countries that the United States viewed as major security threats.[33]

After the disclosure of the Cox committee's findings, Senator Thompson indicated that his own group might hold additional hearings into the charge that China had tried illegally to influence the 1996 election through campaign contributions. The news was "extremely troubling," Thompson indicated.

"But it should come as no surprise to those who have been following our export policies and the activities of the Chinese. It's been well known for some time that China has been actively involved in trying to obtain technology information, and I believe that our policies have played into their efforts."[34]

In 1999, the China connection burst back onto the national agenda when reporters uncovered allegations that the People's Republic "stole nuclear secrets for bombs" through espionage at the Los Alamos Scientific Laboratory in New Mexico.[35] According to the investigation, in the mid-1980s China had taken U.S. information on miniature warheads and used it to develop its own capacity to launch a number of small warheads from a single missile.

Since the spying had taken place before Bill Clinton was elected, no one blamed the Arkansas man for that disaster. Critics did charge, though, that when told of the Chinese spying in the summer of 1997 the White House had not taken the allegations very seriously because of its efforts to open a dialogue with Beijing. One U.S. official pointed out that "this conflicted with their China policy. It undercut the Administration's efforts to have a strategic partnership with the Chinese."[36]

Shortly before the story broke, the Clinton administration fired a Chinese-American scientist, Wen Ho Lee, who worked at Los Alamos after he failed a polygraph test.[37] But congressional critics demanded more information. Curt Weldon, a Pennsylvania Republican, said, "They're trying to spin this thing to get the best play for themselves and avoid further embarrassment. They want to drag it out as long as they can. I'm so mad I can't see straight."[38]

When asked about the matter, Clinton denied any impropriety. "We did not ignore evidence. Quite the contrary, we acted on it," he said.[39] He went on to point out that U.S. involvement with China was good policy because it helped to integrate the world's most populous country into the international order.

Outside observers were not persuaded. The *New York Times* columnist William Safire suggested that the president went soft on the Chinese because "they raised millions for the Clinton campaign."[40] Encouraged by the big contributor James Riady, the White House had eased trade restrictions on satellites and computers. Clinton did not want detailed scrutiny of the alleged spying activities for fear it would damage his China opening, critics charged.

Such claims gained some credence when Johnny Chung, a former Democratic fundraiser, admitted "that he had funneled tens of thousands of dollars from two high-level Chinese military officials to President Clinton's re-election effort in 1996."[41] According to newspaper accounts, Chung informed Justice Department investigators as part of a plea bargain that General Ji Shengde, chief of China's military intelligence agency, had wired $300,000 to Chung's account for use in Clinton's campaign and that Chung gave $35,000 of that amount to the president's re-election fund.

Chung had long been of interest to congressional officials. An old friend of Clinton's from Arkansas and a frequent White House visitor, he had become controversial during the campaign for his $400,000 donations to the Democratic National Committee and the Clinton re-election fund, money that party officials later returned, since contributions from overseas governments were expressly prohibited in American political races. No one wanted foreign officials financing U.S. elections, given the potential for blatant conflicts of interest.

Chung also testified that his business partner, Liu Chao-ying, an aerospace executive and lieutenant colonel in the People's Liberation Army, had bragged to him that the Clinton fundraisers Charlie Yah Lin Trie and John Huang were "directed in their fund-raising activities by the Chinese government."[42] These charges and the damaging trail of foreign money they exposed remained the most troubling element of the 1996 campaign finance controversy.

Conclusion

The 1996 Democratic fundraising scandal illustrates a fundamental risk hanging over future elections. As overseas mergers and acquisitions propelled by the forces of globalization further blur the boundaries between U.S. and foreign corporations, the problem of illegal contributions from overseas is likely to get more severe. The growing interconnections of the international economy make it more and more difficult to police gifts from abroad, especially in the case of countries whose banking laws lie outside the realm of U.S. investigations.

The scandal also demonstrates the political risks of the Democrats' response. The White House shielded itself from the worst of the political backlash by engaging in careful spin control and by implying Republicans were also involved in financial irregularities, even though no evidence ever documented that candidate Dole had broken fundraising laws. Although Clinton won re-election in 1996, he and his party paid a price in the bad feelings that emerged and which contributed to the partisan rancor that marked the impeachment controversy. Republicans felt the president had intentionally deceived them on the fund-raising charges and that he could not be trusted. Such feelings encouraged the GOP to pursue the Lewinsky scandal with relish.

This sequence of events illustrates how important the rules of the game are to American politics. Politicians must have faith that the opponents are playing by the same rules as they are. Otherwise, there is no trust, and that is damaging to the system as a whole.

Following the letter and spirit of the law is especially important in regard to campaign finance. Money is so essential to electioneering that the question of how it is acquired and used deserves unusual care. Financing is vital to electoral strategies and communications, and it sharply influences who does well with voters. If one party unfairly gains an advantage, it weakens support for the political system and creates ill will all around.

By pushing the envelope much further than it had ever been pushed, the Democratic National Committee set a bad precedent for future elections. It created a vast reservoir of mistrust in the opposition party, which had policy consequences. When the dust had settled, the whole controversy over unethical campaign fundraising left a legacy that will stain the American political system for years to come.

CHAPTER 6

The Teamsters and
the Clinton White House

IT WAS A SHORT ANSWER to a seemingly innocuous question on the third day of a legal deposition. Interviewed on September 22, 1997, by a Senate Governmental Affairs Committee attorney as part of the investigation into campaign fundraising, former White House deputy chief of staff Harold Ickes was asked what Clinton personnel had done during a Teamsters' strike at a Stockton, California, plant owned by Diamond Walnut Growers. "Nothing that I know of," Ickes replied.[1]

From the standpoint of the White House staffer and chief liaison to the DNC and the campaign organization, that was the truth. He had been deposed in various legal proceedings twenty-six times, more than anyone else in the Clinton administration. The incessant questioning was wearing on him. It was one of many reasons Ickes despised the Republicans. A dyed-in-the-wool liberal who was the son of a celebrated member of Franklin Roosevelt's administration, Ickes believed Republicans were engaged in a witch-hunt against Democrats and that he was merely a pawn in the larger game.

Before he joined the White House, Ickes had been the object of a federal probe into his legal work for a union thought to be infiltrated by organized crime. His specialty was labor law, and much of his career had centered on unions in one form or another, so it was not unusual that he was being asked about a long-running strike.

Nothing came of the federal investigation into his work for the union, and in January 1994 Ickes joined the administration as deputy chief of staff. He loved being in the White House. It was the center of the action in American politics, a position from which one could help friends and harm enemies. Ickes served in the White House until November 1996, when he was unceremoniously removed by a new chief of staff.

As far as he knew, the White House had not been involved with the Teamsters' labor dispute. His testimony clearly indicated that. However, the statement would soon pose problems for him. The entire case would raise a host of questions about how the Clinton administration raised money.

The International Brotherhood of Teamsters

One of the largest unions in the United States, with 1.4 million members, the Teamsters had long been involved in politics. Ever since the days when the legendary Jimmy Hoffa ran the union, sometimes with the aid of organized crime, the Teamsters had appreciated how public officials could help or hinder labor in reaching its goals. From issues surrounding organizing activities to rules governing strikes, the union realized government could have a dramatic impact on its actions.

For much of the labor movement, the central thrust of political activism centered on the Democratic party, traditionally thought to be more sympathetic to its concerns. Unions contributed money, provided volunteers, and otherwise supported Democrats running for office. It had been that way since the 1930s, when New Dealers had used the government to help workers organize against unfair conditions.

The members of the Teamsters were the only real exception. Unlike their colleagues, they often supported Republican candidates. Hoffa, for example, the union's leader from 1957 to 1971, had endorsed Nixon for president. Other union locals had worked on behalf of Reagan in the 1980s.

Ever since Robert Kennedy's sharp attacks on their leadership when he was counsel to the Senate's McClellan Committee in the late 1950s, the Teamsters harbored no lost love for the Democratic party. Less ideological and more pragmatic than other labor groups, the union liked to go with whatever party or candidate offered the best deal. It was a strategy that had garnered major benefits over the years.

Part of the Teamsters' antipathy to other bodies in the labor movement stemmed from its own unique history. Having been infiltrated by organized crime, it was expelled from the AFL-CIO in 1959 and became an independent union. Persistent federal corruption probes led to the conviction of several of the organization's presidents. In 1983, Roy Williams was sentenced to prison on conspiracy charges. His successor, Jackie Presser, was indicted in 1986 for embezzlement and racketeering. Three of the last six Teamsters presidents had gone to prison.

The union was renowned for some of the most undemocratic rules of any labor group in America. Its membership conventions, for example, were held only once every five years. Presidents were paid high salaries and had the power to appoint persons to a large number of positions within the union hierarchy. Dissidents were often physically ejected from meetings. Top leaders were elected at the convention, rather than by the membership as a whole in a mail ballot. This tended to favor those already in charge of the union.

The Teamsters would not rejoin the AFL-CIO until October 1987.[2] A year later, the Reagan administration put the union into receivership, with government-appointed overseers. This decision would sour its association with the GOP. By the early 1990s, the organization was edging back to a closer relationship with the Democratic party. After a decade of union bashing from the Republicans, the time seemed ripe for a new alliance.

The Walnut Growers' Strike

Against the backdrop of these political maneuverings a major labor dispute erupted. On September 4, 1991, at the height of the harvest season, nearly three hundred persons who worked at a Diamond Walnut processing plant in Stockton, California, walked off the job. The company, a cooperative owned by two thousand walnut growers, was not being fair, according to the workers.

A few years before, when the company had fallen on hard times, workers at Teamsters Local 601 had taken a 30 to 40 percent pay cut in their $10 hourly wage. Two-thirds of those who worked at the company were women, and most of them now were making $6 to $7 an hour.[3] The employees had not wanted to accept the pay reductions, but they felt their jobs and the long-term financial health of the company were at stake.

The cooperative had installed automated machinery to process the walnuts. This new technology had cut the workforce in half. New laser equipment automatically separated parts of the walnut, a job previously done by workers. The company went on to post record profits.[4]

Unhappy with their labor situation, the workers had decided to go on strike. The company was doing much better than it had in 1985, the time of the massive pay cut. That year, Diamond Walnut had revenue of $204 million, with profits of between $5 million and $6 million; by 1991, its profits had doubled to $11.2 million. The company was the largest of its kind in the world, delivering 200,000 tons of walnuts to its customers each year.

Yet despite Diamond's prosperity, workers were not sharing in the wealth. The cooperative had raised pay by about $1 an hour over the preceding few years, but this still was 20 to 30 percent below the 1985 rate. The union wanted a new pay boost of $1 per hour; the company was offering raises of only 10¢ an hour and, if profits were good, annual bonuses ranging up to a few thousand dollars.[5]

Consistent with the efforts of many businesses during this period to get a handle on the cost of health benefits, Diamond was demanding that employees pay a portion of their health insurance, around $33 per month for the typical worker. In conjunction with reduced wages and high profits, this seemed utterly indefensible to the Teamsters.

A strike was called and workers took to the picket lines.

Employees who walked out received $200 a week in union strikers' benefits. This was half what they had made when they were working.

Rather than sit back and wait for the strike to be settled, the company took decisive action. It was, after all, the middle of harvest season. As one of Diamond's managers explained, "The strike occurred at our peak harvest time. We had to hire people or we wouldn't have made it through the season."[6] The walkout came at a time when unions represented only 12 percent of workers in the United States, down from 25 percent a decade earlier.

Emboldened by gains anti-union forces had made during the 1980s, and with new federal labor laws enacted during the Reagan administration at its disposal, the company decided to hire permanent replacement workers, many of them young men, to supplant its predominantly female labor force. These new employees processed the harvest, and many stayed on as permanent laborers.

As the months and then years passed by, this labor dispute became one of the longest and most bitter strikes in the United States. In most cases, the company refused to rehire those who had lost their jobs. For the union, the strike became a litmus test of how politicians were handling the new economy that was emerging in the United States.

The Clinton White House

Sensing an opportunity for a mutually beneficial partnership, the Clinton administration entered into talks with Teamsters' officials, who wanted help with the long-running strike against Diamond Walnut and other union matters. A new, reform president was in charge of the labor group, a man named Ron Carey. He had filled his leadership with Democratic-leaning activists. His mission to clean up the union's tawdry public image, eliminate ties to organized crime, and govern in a more democratic manner.

Carey was proud of the progress he had made since taking charge in 1991. He had cut his own salary, sold the union's jets, and broken up with local fiefdoms. "We've taken some real dramatic steps. We've put together an ethical practices committee with rank and file members. I've put trusteeships into four or more local unions. We're putting together a compliance manual with new rules and regulations. We've done some unique things that haven't been done in 88 years."[7]

The new labor leader had one other thing going for him. He was an early and strong backer of Bill Clinton. Campaigning for the Democrat in 1992, Carey had publicly praised the candidate and extolled his virtues to the union. When Clinton won the presidency, Carey had a close friend in the White House. Since then, and in contrast to earlier days, most of the union's $10 million in political contributions had gone to Democrats.[8]

The Diamond Walnut strike really bothered Carey. The company's ability to break the strike by hiring permanent replacement workers illustrated for him exactly what was wrong with the new economy. The rich were getting richer and the poor were getting poorer. Ordinary workers who did hard physical labor were not appreciated by those who ran companies. "The ability to replace workers who strike is a frightening problem when you hit the bargaining table. I mean, it's like you are behind by 50 percent before you even give management your proposals," he said.[9]

Carey resolved to use his newfound political connections to help him on a variety of issues. There was the difficult labor-organizing effort at Pony Express, an Atlanta package delivery company. The union also wanted the administration to delay a NAFTA rule allowing Mexican truck drivers to deliver goods anywhere in the United States (the White House did so, as a favor to Carey).

And the Diamond Walnut strike had no end in sight. In October 1993, less than a year into the Clinton administration, a report by the Department of Labor condemned the company. According to its author, Karen Nussbaum, director of the department's Women's Bureau, Diamond Walnut had abandoned its employees while enjoying record profits. Workers "thought they would be compensated for their contribution when the company's economic health improved." That had not happened. When employees had demanded their fair share by going on strike, management had replaced them. In Nussbaum's view, "[H]iring permanent replacements causes extensive damage to workers and their communities."[10]

The scathing report came out a day before employees were to vote on decertifying the Teamsters Union as their representative. A member of Congress found the timing suspicious. "This [report] was a further politicization of the federal bureaucracy," stated Representative Richard Pombo, a California Republican.[11] A company official, Vice President Richard Douglas, held a similar view. "There's no doubt in my mind that the report was part of an orchestrated public relations campaign," he remarked. In the end, the release of the document did not help the union. By a 592 to 366 vote, the striking workers decertified the Teamsters.

But the National Labor Relations Board ruled that the company had used unfair labor practices to influence the election. It ordered another vote in 1993, which also went against the union, this time by a margin of 575 to 475. Again, the NLRB found fault with Diamond Walnut. Even though they had received only low-paying positions, the company had reinstated three striking workers right before the election. The Teamsters argued this had a chilling effect on other employees, and that the vote therefore was illegal.[12]

The Fundraising Investigation by Congress

Several years after the NLRB's decision, the Senate Governmental Affairs Committee was looking into how money was raised during Clinton's 1996 campaign. There were questions about contributions from foreign sources. Republicans in particular were worried about money from companies with ties to the Chinese government.

Along the way to examining foreign gifts, however, investigators noticed some odd activities involving the Teamsters and the White House. Big contributions for Clinton's re-election had come in from the union. That in itself, of course, was not illegal. But more troubling was possible intervention in Teamsters' labor disputes, particularly the protracted Diamond Walnut Growers strike. Committee lawyers were concerned that members of the administration had traded government actions for contributions.

In his September 22, 1997, deposition, Harold Ickes had denied any knowledge of White House involvement in the strike. When asked about this directly, he had answered, "Nothing that I know of." The long-time labor activist had testified under oath that the White House had not taken action in the dispute.

However, investigators for the committee had unearthed evidence to the contrary. For starters, there had been a June 17, 1996, lunch at the executive mansion, just four days before the Teamsters contributed $236,000 to various state Democratic parties around the country.[13]

Interviews with participants revealed that there had been detailed planning to arrange an illegal swap of contributions. In return for Teamsters' donations to Clinton, the Democratic National Committee would help raise money for Ron Carey's tough 1996 re-election effort. At this point, the union's president was under siege. As the reformist leader of a labor group with a troubled history, he had alienated the old guard with his emphasis on change. Nor did they like it when he put several local affiliates into formal receivership and revoked local rule.

These traditionalist elements within the union had found the ideal opponent to challenge Carey: James P. Hoffa, Jr., the son of the former Teamsters' president. The two men were locked in a very tight race that ultimately would see Carey prevail by a margin of 50.5 to 49.5 percent. For their own separate reasons, Carey and Clinton needed each other desperately.

Several men already had pleaded guilty to charges that money had been laundered between the two campaigns. Martin

Davis, a Teamsters' political consultant, found out in mid-1996 that the union planned to make major contributions to Democratic candidates. Ever the creative fundraiser, he hatched a plan to employ the gift as "a means to induce the DNC to raise money for the Carey campaign."[14]

In conversations with the Democratic National Committee, Davis proposed that in return for the party locating someone willing to give $100,000 to Carey, the Teamsters would donate $1 million for Clinton and the DNC. Following a June 1996 lunch, an official at the committee sent Davis a letter outlining which state party organizations should receive contributions.

In return, DNC fundraisers found a Philippine woman willing to contribute $100,000 to Carey. She had wanted to make the gift to the DNC, but was ineligible to do so as a foreign national. So the party put her in touch with the Teamsters, who directed that the money be laundered through Vote Now '96, a non-profit organization in Florida. Her donation was to be accompanied by explicit instructions, communicated in writing, labeling it "Vote '96 underwriting Teamsters."[15]

The arrangement was not limited to this contribution swap. The Teamsters also wanted direct help with the Diamond Walnut Growers strike, which had now dragged on for half a decade. A March 1995 memo from the White House aide Jennifer O'Connor to her boss, Harold Ickes, noted: "It is in our best interest to develop a better relationship with Carey. . . . We are in a good position to rekindle the Teamster leadership's enthusiasm for the Administration. A meeting (with Clinton) would be a good idea and could help Carey." In particular, she noted, the White House "should assist in any way possible" with the

Diamond Walnut strike and the organizing effort at Pony Express in Atlanta.[16]

Around that same time, the Teamsters' political director, Bill Hamilton, informed union leaders he had been told by administration officials that the White House would intervene in the two labor disputes. A year later, the union and the DNC worked out the contribution swap.

In a speech at the National Press Club, Ron Carey claimed he had no knowledge of the illegal activity that had resulted in guilty pleas by three of his aides. "You cannot know all of the things that go on in a big organization. You hire people that are trusted, people who are competent, people who will do the job, and you put your trust in them. And as usual, human nature being what it is, people step over the line."[17]

A federal judge disagreed with this benign interpretation. In 1997, Carey's election was ruled null and void because of the illegal money laundering and embezzlement of union funds involved in helping re-elect him. According to the magistrate, as much as $700,000 of Carey's $2 million campaign fund, more than one-third of the total, had come from illegal sources. Some of this money was raised in conjunction with efforts made on behalf of the union by the DNC and the White House.[18] Eventually, Carey would be disqualified from seeking re-election and Hoffa would win the resulting 1998 special vote.

The Senate was interested in Ickes' involvement with the Diamond Walnut strike. His own aide, Jennifer O'Connor, had testified that Ickes had asked the U.S. trade representative, Mickey Kantor, to call Diamond Walnut's president, William

Cuff, to see if the company would settle the dispute. Republicans on the panel concluded that Ickes had given "less than candid testimony."[19] O'Connor was asked to follow up and ensure Kantor made the phone call.[20] A Teamsters' memo indicated that Kantor "agreed to use his discretionary authority to try to convince the CEO of that company [Diamond Walnut] that they should settle the dispute."[21]

Even worse, from the standpoint of congressional investigators, was that they had unearthed a previously undisclosed memo from Ickes to Kantor. It informed the trade representative that Ickes had met with a group of Teamsters leaders and that the deputy chief of staff was anxious to talk face-to-face with Kantor about the strike. "Given the situation I would like to meet with you at your very earliest possible convenience to discuss this situation," he wrote. Ickes then met with Kantor on March 24, 1995, and sent a thank-you note on March 27. On April 4, Kantor called Cuff, the president of Diamond Walnut, to discuss the importance of resolving the strike.[22] According to Kantor, in his call he asked "for an update and what are the prospects for settlement." The trade representative testified that he "considered the call benign, part of my job and of no great consequence."[23]

Cuff, however, had a far different reaction. Testifying before the House Subcommittee on Oversight and Investigation, the business executive said he never before had gotten a phone call from a high-ranking administration official. The call made him nervous, and he reported it to his board. "There was absolutely no explicit threat. The only thing I would say is that when you get a call from a senior official of the Administration you have to be concerned. I figured it was part of the ongoing significant effort by the union to try to bring us to our knees."[24]

The Justice Department Investigation

Attorney General Janet Reno was not sure what to make of the Ickes case. Republicans were pressing her to appoint yet another independent counsel. Key GOP officials thought that both Clinton and Gore had violated key provisions of the Federal Election Campaign Act in the 1996 election. Reno demurred, however, and chose not to prosecute either case.

The Ickes matter, though, was more disturbing. Justice Department officials had been investigating the allegations for months, and they were torn. On the one hand, they hated to suggest appointing an independent counsel. Ken Starr's aggressive pursuit of the president on Whitewater, the Lewinsky affair, and other matters had tainted the office and made the attorney general quite cautious about calling for the appointment of another such individual with an open-ended mandate to hunt for evidence.

Yet congressional testimony and the documentary trail appeared to tie Ickes to illegal fundraising, at the least. Three officials in the Teamsters Union had already pleaded guilty on this charge. The question confronting her was whether Ickes had lied on September 22, 1997, in his deposition for the Senate Governmental Affairs Committee. The committee clearly thought so. Its final report concluded that he had "misled its investigators about his actions on behalf of the International Brotherhood of Teamsters."[25]

Reno's own top aide, Charles La Bella, as well as officials from the Federal Bureau of Investigation had urged her to call for an independent counsel. In a report summarizing his own investigation of Ickes, La Bella had argued there was additional unpublished evidence implicating him and that an independent counsel should be requested.[26] To do otherwise, he felt, would undermine the requirement for honest testimony before congressional investigators.

On January 29, 1999, in a letter thirty-six pages long, Reno announced her decision. She had considered the case for ninety days and then sought a sixty-day extension. Following this review, she would not ask for the appointment of an independent counsel to investigate the White House link to the Teamsters. After analyzing the evidence, the attorney general concluded that "there are no reasonable grounds to investigate further whether Ickes committed perjury, because I believe that there is clear and convincing evidence that Ickes's testimony, even if false, was not knowingly and willfully so."[27]

"The questions asked of Ickes," she added, "were ambiguous, and his answers were truthful under a reasonable interpretation of the question. The serious defects in the questioning, the relatively insignificant nature of the underlying event, the extended lapse of time, and the absence of any perceivable motive to conceal create an insurmountable barrier to the proof of any potential criminal violation."[28]

Republicans, predictably, were outraged. Senator Orrin Hatch, chairman of the Judiciary Committee, said, "[F]rankly there's enough evidence that should have triggered the independent counsel statute. It's a very grave disappointment." Congressman Dan Burton was even more pointed in his criticism: "The attorney general is once again protecting the President and his friends. Janet Reno has defied the spirit and the letter of the independent counsel statute. Her investigation has become a sham."[29]

Conclusion

Despite the exoneration of Ickes, the illegal swap of contributions between the Teamsters and the Democratic National Committee illustrates just one more way in which current campaign finance rules are being flouted. Unusual because of the specificity of the evidence documenting the arrangement and the cavalier manner in which the plan was implemented, this case shows how unfair fundraising practices have policy consequences.

With the large amounts of secret money floating around the political system and the nearly insatiable needs of candidates for contributions, the only thing that is surprising is that such examples do not arise more frequently. The permeability of the American political process and the necessity of bringing in money produce a natural link between contributors and officials who do favors in order to advance their fundraising.

Obviously, the Clinton administration does not provide the only example of suspicious campaign finance practices. For example, critics frequently charged Bob Dole with delivering favorable tax breaks for Archer Daniels Midland, the Gallo family, and the Koch family of Kansas in return for substantial contributions.

In regard to the latter, with estimated annual revenues of $25 billion and business interests spanning oil, real estate, and livestock, Koch Industries long was a top donor to the Kansas Republican. In 1995 the company gave Dole $245,000, making it his third-largest contributor.[30] Koch officials also helped the senator raise money for other causes.

In 1989, the company was accused of stealing oil from Native American reservations. According to a report by the Senate Select Committee on Indian Affairs, Koch Industries stole oil from tribal lands "by deliberately undermeasuring and underreporting how much it took." After Dole pressured the committee's staff to water down the report, a grand jury dropped its investigation in 1992.[31]

Executives of the Archer Daniels Midland Company, meanwhile, not only contributed to Dole's campaigns, but also made generous donations to the American Red Cross, headed by the senator's wife, Elizabeth Dole. According to news reports, Dwayne Andeas, longtime head of the company, made at least $3 million in gifts to the Red Cross after Elizabeth Dole became its president in 1991. As a senator, Bob Dole was a champion of the ethanol industry, supporting tax breaks that were of financial interest to the agribusiness conglomerate.[32]

Dole is not alone in helping favored business leaders. Newt Gingrich, formerly Speaker of the House, had an unusually close relationship with the textile magnate Roger Milliken. He gave hundreds of thousands of dollars to Gingrich's political action committee, GOPAC, and Gingrich always was eager to protect textile manufacturers. Indeed, the Speaker broker with his own party's opposition to import quotas to lobby for action insulating the textile industry from a flood of cheap foreign goods.[33]

Such reciprocity is so difficult to document because it generally takes place in secret, outside the realm of public disclosure and media attention. If government officials are careful in their statements and circumspect about what they put down on paper, campaign finance rules are so vague as to pose little threat of prosecution. Only when plans are well documented do cases come to light and create legal and political problems for public officials.

CHAPTER 7

Big Tobacco
and the Republican
National Committee

S EVEN CHIEF EXECUTIVES of tobacco companies stood in front of the House Energy and Commerce Subcommittee on Health and the Environment on April 14, 1994, swearing an oath to tell the truth. They were the most powerful men in the industry, with the leaders of Philip Morris, R. J. Reynolds, and Brown and Williamson among their number. Most of them made annual salaries of several million dollars.

For six hours they were asked a series of tough questions about smoking. How were the levels of nicotine in cigarettes set? What about advertising aimed at young people? What of unpublished research concerning the effects of tobacco on those who smoked?[1]

Without exception, the men toed the industry line on the question of health risks. Tobacco might be linked to cancer, emphysema, and heart disease, they testified, but the evidence was "not conclusive."[2] James Johnston, the head of R. J. Reynolds, noted that "all products, from cola to Twinkies, had risks associated with them." That might be true, replied the subcommittee's chairman, Henry Waxman, a California Democrat, "but the difference between cigarettes and Twinkies is death."

Andrew Tisch, chairman of the Lorillard Tobacco Company, was asked if he knew cigarettes caused cancer. "I do not believe that. . . . We have looked at the data [they do] not convince me that smoking causes death," he responded, contradicting what many members of the general public believed.[3]

None of the men testifying thought that cigarettes were addictive. The chief executives denied that their businesses "spike cigarettes with extra nicotine to hook smokers."[4] Each strenuously argued that their companies should not be held liable for any health damage attendant to smoking. Any such penalties would not be fair and would violate the spirit of our free enterprise system.

The tobacco executives' testimony would mark the beginning of a major challenge for their industry. Opinion polls showed the public was turning against the business. More and more persons were lining up behind the antismoking movement. Political leaders were being asked to pass sharp new restrictions on the sale and use of their product. The long-term survival of the tobacco industry was in question.

And there were other major problems. The Food and Drug Administration was clamoring for tough controls on tobacco. Cities and states were passing antismoking legislation covering restaurants, workplaces, and other public areas. Court decisions were starting to blame tobacco products for illness and death. Juries of ordinary citizens were becoming less sympathetic to their business.

Yet the industry was not dead. Big tobacco would live on to fight against being regulated and being held liable for a variety of medical ailments. For it had something public officials desperately needed—the ability to take to the airwaves as an ally and lots of money for campaign contributions. In fact, the industry would fare better than many critics believed was possible.

The Health Risks of Smoking

The case against tobacco products took years to build. First presented in obscure medical journals, the evidence slowly seeped out to the general public. Cigarettes were hazardous to human health in a variety of ways. Smoking was dangerous to women during pregnancy. It was a major risk factor for developing heart disease and emphysema. Tobacco products were strongly associated with lung cancer.

As early as 1941, Dr. Michael DeBakey, who later gained fame for pioneering artificial-heart transplants, published an article noting an odd correlation. As tobacco sales went up, lung cancer increased as well. A decade later, the scientists Ernst Wynder and Evarts Graham published an article which documented that "96.5 percent of lung-cancer patients are moderate-to-heavy smokers." This was followed in rapid succession by another Wynder study demonstrating that "painting cigarette tar on the backs of mice creates tumors."[5] Damning evidence was starting to build.

For years, tobacco companies played down the science behind these findings. The studies, they said, were based mainly on correlational research. Causation should not be assumed.

The mere fact that two things like smoking and lung cancer were statistically associated did not definitely prove that tobacco was the culprit. Other factors might account for the health risks, they proclaimed. People who smoked also had other bad health habits. Their diets were poor and they failed to get sufficient exercise.

But more and more studies documented the serious risks posed by smoking. In 1964, Surgeon General Luther Terry became the first federal official to warn about the health hazards connected with tobacco smoking. It was a risk about which the public needed to learn.

A year later, Congress passed the Federal Cigarette Labeling and Advertising Act. This legislation placed an official warning from the surgeon general on cigarette packs and cartons noting that smoking could be hazardous to health.[6] It was the first time the government had singled out the tobacco industry for such a warning.

In 1982, Surgeon General Everett Koop published a report suggesting that secondhand smoke might cause lung cancer. It took eight years, but in 1990 the government banned smoking on domestic passenger flights under six hours in length because of such concerns. Persons did not have to use tobacco themselves to be vulnerable; just being around smokers was a hazard.

It had been nearly fifty years since DeBakey's original research, but, slowly, the noose was tightening around the industry. A series of lawsuits holding tobacco companies liable for deaths and disease was making its way through the courts in the 1990s. As part of the legal discovery process, incriminating documents were being made public. Whistle-blowers within the industry were turning over evidence to lawyers and reporters alleging that companies knew more than their chief executives let on.

One source of such information was Jeffrey Wigand, Brown and Williamson's vice president for research and development from 1989 to 1993. Wigand's job, which paid $400,000 a year, put him in the know. A wide range of sensitive company documents and research studies flowed across his desk. In a February 1996 interview on CBS's *60 Minutes* he "accused Brown and Williamson's [chief executive Thomas] Sandefur of lying to Congress in 1994 when he testified, along with other tobacco chief executives, that he did not believe nicotine was addictive."[7]

Legal depositions given by Wigand in 1996 also accused his former employer of using chemicals in its cigarettes "to enhance the effects of nicotine," of shipping sensitive research overseas to prevent litigants from seeing it, and "of opposing work on safer cigarettes to avoid legal liability."[8]

Merrell Williams worked at a Louisville law firm, Wyatt Tarrant and Combs, from 1989 to 1992. His job took him to Brown and Williamson, where he kept track of documents and research relevant to tobacco litigation. Increasingly aggrieved at what he saw, Williams secretly copied four thousand pages of damaging internal company documents and turned them over to opponents of smoking.

Among the information they revealed was that, as early as 1963, Brown and Williamson's lawyers had informed the firm that "it is in the business of selling an addictive drug, and its research scientists have reported for years that the product can pose serious health risks for users."[9]

The final straw came in 1996. Ian Uydess, a researcher at Philip Morris, revealed in a Food and Drug Administration deposition that his company "shelved his findings on how to remove poisonous nitrates from tobacco, [and] then muzzled other scientists who were examining nicotine's addictive nature."[10] A body of evidence had accumulated that tobacco firms had been aware for decades that their product was carcinogenic. Company scientists testified they had warned of the dangers to health, but were told to keep their mouths shut. This dark secret had been known only to a small group of persons in the tobacco business.

Political Risks Facing the Industry

With the accumulating evidence of the major health costs of smoking, the federal government started to become more active. At first, the strategy had centered on warning labels. Disclosure was the key, not regulation. Smokers could not be told not to inhale. That would only drive tobacco use underground, as Prohibition had done with alcohol in the 1920s. Regulation did not appear to be an effective approach.

But consumers should be made aware of what a growing body of scientific research had uncovered. Cigarettes should be labeled with a warning telling consumers that smoking could be hazardous to their health. That way, at least, persons could make an informed decision regarding health risks.

The tobacco companies, of course, had fought even this minimalist approach. The science documenting medical problems was imperfect and incomplete, they claimed. Industry groups cited the specter of big government interfering with the private marketplace in their objections to disclosure requirements. It was unfair to single them out for a crackdown.

But their complaints went for naught. In 1965, over the protests of tobacco-state legislators, Congress had mandated that warning labels be placed on cigarette packs. By 1971, Congress had banned cigarette advertising on television and radio. In 1973, no-smoking sections were required on domestic flights.[11]

In the years following these decisions, more research came out documenting the dangers of cigarette smoking, whether from direct or secondhand exposure. Congress began to consider new kinds of regulations. Disclosure was having only a modest impact on deaths associated with smoking. By 1990, it was estimated that 400,000 men and women were dying every year from tobacco-associated illnesses. Every day, nearly 3,000 young people were starting to smoke. Over time, 1,000 of them would end up dead as a result of their tobacco habit.[12]

Antismoking advocates started to move toward urging outright bans. The first target was air travel. Although airlines had separate sections for smokers and nonsmokers, in a small, airtight plane it was virtually impossible to keep smoke from drifting throughout the cabin. In 1990, smoking on short domestic flights was banned.

Then, the battle expanded to restaurants, the workplace, and public buildings. Slowly, both Congress and state legislatures were extending the smoking bans to more and more areas. What had begun as a requirement to have separate sections for smokers and nonsmokers was now moving toward outright prohibition.

In 1994 the commissioner of the U.S. Food and Drug Administration, David Kessler, was exploring whether tobacco could be regulated by declaring nicotine a drug. According to Kessler, "[T]he definition of a drug is an article intended to affect the structure and function of the body. You can go to a library and find out that nicotine does that. The question was, did the companies intend that."[13]

The next year, President Clinton announced his support for the FDA move regulating tobacco. The transformation was nearly complete. Government would take an aggressive approach toward tobacco companies. Much like prescription medications, tobacco would be regulated as a hazardous product.

The Public Relations Strategy

Throughout the decades when evidence was accumulating about the health risks associated with tobacco products, the industry had devised a clever public relations strategy to build goodwill. It was not financially wise to be known as a death business. So the tobacco companies began to do good deeds.

Philanthropy was one major undertaking. Cigarette companies gave financial support to universities, museums, concerts, and other cultural institutions and activities. In fact, these corporations were among the top underwriters of a wide range of charitable activities. In 1995 alone, Philip Morris, Brown and Williamson, and R. J. Reynolds contributed over $265,000 to the American Red Cross, headed by Elizabeth Dole, to help the victims of natural disasters.[14]

Sports sponsorships also became a top priority. There were, for example, Philip Morris race cars, tennis matches, and golf tournaments. Each year, tobacco companies put on the Tournament Players Championship for professional golfers at a private course in Potomac, Maryland. Again, the goal was the same: present the firms in the most positive light and in the most favorable venues possible.

The tobacco industry published magazines that provided a forum for research that was to its liking. Major companies devoted nearly a million dollars to the magazine *Healthy Buildings,* which promoted tobacco interests. Often relying on suspect science, this publication actively protested the idea that bans on indoor smoking were necessary to maintain good health.

Accompanying these public relations efforts were research activities, all of which sponsored projects having a pro-industry point of view. For example, the law firm Covington and Burling, which had long represented leading tobacco companies, supported a major study in 1996 that concluded federal restrictions on tobacco would cost America ninety-two thousand lost jobs and $7.9 billion in lost sales.[15] This and other slanted works were merely one way in which big tobacco attempted to communicate its point of view to the general public.

Political Contributions

Philanthropy, sponsorships, and biased journalism might be fine for ordinary citizens, but legislators required something more tangible: money, and lots of it. Tobacco companies knew that it cost a lot to win elections in the television era. Making, not to mention running, all those ads was very expensive. Incumbents, and sometimes challengers, needed to finance their races, and the industry was only too eager to help out.

Cigarette companies were among the country's most generous makers of direct donations to candidates. Millions of dollars each year went to women and men who were running for Congress or the presidency, each contribution designed to provide access. Tobacco had traditionally been bipartisan in its campaign contributions, with gifts flowing evenly to Republican and Democratic candidates. It made sense to spread the money around to both parties. However, when the GOP won the House and the Senate in 1994, tobacco shifted toward a more partisan strategy. Accordingly, between 1993 and 1995 the industry donated $4.5 million to Republicans and $800,000 to Democrats, according to the Federal Election Commission.[16]

The goal was not just persuasion, but access. Lobbyists for cigarette companies wanted to make sure they had a seat at the table when controversial rules were debated. Although such gifts never guaranteed success, they typically allowed industry executives to have their voices heard in the debate, at least with the dominant party in Congress.

Soft-money contributions to the two parties were another way tobacco interests attempted to sway the political process. In 1997, for example, cigarette makers donated around $2 million to the national committees for general party-building activities. Of this, the vast preponderance went to the GOP: $1.6 million, compared to $400,000 for the Democrats.[17] Philip Morris was among the largest donors, at nearly $800,000. These sums

were higher than in preceding years. For example, in 1988 cigarette companies donated $448,000 to the GOP in soft-money
gifts, and $38,000 to the Democrats; the corresponding figures
for 1992 were $1.34 million and $731,000, respectively.[18]

Direct, personal contact was another form of influence ped-
dling. By one estimate, in 1997 the industry devoted nearly $30
million to lobbying government officials.[19] This included money
spent on expensive Washington offices, well-placed lawyers, and
public relations strategists. Moreover, each year the Tobacco
Institute sponsored a legislative conference that attracted two
dozen members of Congress. Held at the Hyatt Grand Champi-
ons Resort in Palm Springs, California, the weekend meeting
featured free lodging, food, and entertainment for the legislators. For participating in one of the institute's panel discussions,
members earned $2,000 in speaking fees (before the House and
Senate banned such honoraria). Legislators also received book-
lets summarizing tobacco issues facing the upcoming Congress.[20]

The Court Threat

In August 1996 a historic legal decision shocked the tobacco
industry. A Florida jury awarded $750,000 to Grady Carter, a
private individual who had sued Brown and Williamson for failing to fully inform smokers of the health risks posed by cigarettes. News of the ruling sent industry stocks down sharply. It
was the largest court judgment ever in a health hazard case
involving smoking.[21]

This was not the first lawsuit against big tobacco. In 1994, a national class action suit had been filed against the industry on behalf of smokers who had died from lung cancer. But the case had gone nowhere. Two years later, a federal appeals court had dismissed the lawsuit.[22]

But the general climate was changing. Polls documented that public opinion had shifted dramatically against tobacco. Support for smoking bans had risen in several different arenas: during air travel, in restaurants, and finally in the workplace itself.

Even worse for big tobacco, internal company documents that had been revealed and incriminating public testimony were making the job of defending the industry much more difficult. As indicated by the Carter lawsuit, the courts were becoming less sympathetic, and cigarette companies were starting to lose.

In previous decades, it had been nearly impossible to hold tobacco firms liable; the science was not definitive, and there was little evidence the manufacturers knew their product was hazardous. That, after all, had been the basis of the congressional testimony of the seven tobacco executives in 1994. Nicotine was not addictive, and cigarette makers should not be blamed for health problems that plagued smokers.

Another difficulty was that the strategy of employing generous philanthropy, soft money, and campaign contributions was becoming controversial. Tobacco money was attracting criticism at election time. Prominent officials, such as House Minority Leader Dick Gephardt and Vice President Al Gore, who had once accepted such funds, now were refusing them and criticizing others who took them.

Bob Dole had aroused controversy in the middle of his 1996 presidential campaign when he had stated on national television that nicotine might not be addictive and that Surgeon General Everett Koop's tough stance against tobacco companies had come about because of brainwashing by "the liberal media."[23]

Speaking about nicotine during an interview with Katie Couric on NBC's *Today* program, Dole had proclaimed, "There is a mixed view among scientists and doctors whether it's addictive or not. I'm not certain whether it's addictive." He went on to add that "only people like you in the media [criticize him on tobacco]. You may be violating the FCC regulations by always, you know, sticking up for the Democrats and advertising their line on your show."[24] The comments created days of bad publicity for the Republican nominee, whose views were not in sync with either those of leading scientists or the majority of the people.

However, the biggest threat looming against the tobacco industry was a series of lawsuits by state attorneys general seeking repayment of Medicaid costs for tobacco-related illnesses. Following the lead of Attorney General Mike Moore of Mississippi, who had filed the first such suit in 1994, twenty-two of his colleagues from around the nation had banded together and were aggressively pursuing big tobacco. Many of the whistleblowers who had come forward against the industry did so in the context of this litigation.

In the face of mounting legal bills, there even had been a breach in big tobacco's vaunted unity. The Liggett Group, the smallest and weakest of the major companies, announced in March 1997 that it would cooperate with the state attorneys general. It was a stunning defection. Not only was Liggett voluntarily turning over sensitive internal documents to the prosecutors, but it agreed "that the industry targets minors and knows nicotine is addictive."[25] According to one former attorney general, James Tierney of Maine, Liggett's admission turned the subject of tobacco "radioactive" in Congress.

In June 1997, a staggering new agreement was announced between the tobacco companies and the forty states that were by then suing them. In the largest settlement ever in a court case, the industry agreed to pay $368.5 billion over twenty-five years and to accept tough new rules regulating tobacco products and advertising. Among other things, the agreement would "acknowledge the government's authority to regulate nicotine, repay billions of dollars to the states for smoking-related health care costs, and fund free stop-smoking programs for whoever wants them." In addition, new warning labels would be placed on cigarette packs and cartons: "WARNING: Smoking can kill you."[26]

In return, government lawsuits against tobacco companies would be illegal in the future, allowing cigarette corporations to save substantially on legal fees. Punitive damage assessments that multiplied the penalties arising from lawsuits were the biggest financial threat to the industry. According to one estimate, tobacco was spending $600 million each year on lawyers' costs. Its overall legal liability was in the billions.[27]

At a press conference announcing the nearly seventy-page settlement, a jubilant Moore predicted, "This agreement will do more for the public health of our nation than all of our lawsuits combined—even if we had all won our individual suits."[28] The only remaining catch was that the pact had to be approved by the White House and by Congress.

Throughout 1997 and 1998, there was enormous pressure on the House and Senate to pass antismoking legislation. It appeared that judgment day had finally arrived for big tobacco. Given the shift in public opinion, the historic settlement with the state attorneys general, and the incriminating documents that had been made public in various lawsuits, many expected the industry to lose this congressional battle. The tide seemed to have turned.

A Surprise Victory

As Congress debated historic legislation to crack down on tobacco products, the companies were in deep trouble. Both Republicans and Democrats were making negative comments. Sharp regulations were being discussed. The industry was set to lose the right to advertise and target young people. Research indicated that "90 percent of adult smokers picked up their habit by the age of 18."[29]

No longer would tobacco be able to use the Marlboro Man, Joe Camel, product placement in movies, and sponsorship of sporting events to advertise products. The proposed legislation would force a radical change in the political and public relations strategy long employed by the industry.

It was estimated that cigarette companies had devoted nearly $50 billion to image enhancement from the mid-1970s to the mid-1990s. R. J. Reynolds alone had spent $30 million a year on sports advertising, such as the Winston Cup Series and other NASCAR events. The Winston brand was the largest single sponsor of auto racing in the United States.[30]

But almost as soon as the agreement was announced, criticism began that it was too soft on tobacco companies. The White House made known its concern about the language regarding the ability of the Food and Drug Administration to regulate nicotine. In 1996, it had announced that agency's authority to do so as part of the campaign against teen smoking. Now, the White House believed the FDA must have complete power to exercise that authority. In addition, the Clinton administration demanded tougher penalties for tobacco companies if the rate of smoking among adolescents did not decline to meet specified targets.[31]

Other critics demanded even tougher action. For example, a former FDA commissioner and a former surgeon general, David Kessler and Everett Koop, released a joint statement saying, "[I]f the level of youth smoking does not go down within two years, there should be much stiffer, punishing penalties and further restrictions on advertising, promotions and marketing practices."[32] Koop also cautioned that "the tobacco companies are a sleazy bunch of people who misled us, deceived us and lied to us for three decades. Under this settlement, the Tobacco Institute will be gone, but the tobacco lobby will still be there. And they will never stop."[33]

Emboldened by such outside critics, congressional Democrats pushed to make the bill harsher on the industry. This was a once-in-a-lifetime opportunity to tackle a business when political conditions were ripe. They were not going to blow this one.

Senator Orrin Hatch, a Republican of Utah, introduced legislation that followed the broad outlines of the tobacco settlement. He generally was of the belief that the agreement was the best deal that could be reached given the current political situation.

But others did not share this view. The Hatch proposal soon was superseded by a bill championed by another Republican, Senator John McCain of Arizona. Under the McCain proposal, there would be "less legal protection" and "billions more in industry fees."[34] In addition, the federal taxes on cigarettes envisioned in the settlement would be raised from 65¢ to $1.10 a pack. The penalties in the war against tobacco were escalating, and the price tag facing the industry was rising dramatically beyond what had been negotiated with the attorneys general.

Sitting in his corporate headquarters, Steven Goldstone, the chief executive officer of RJR Nabisco, was becoming less and less happy. Big tobacco's "prime strategist," Goldstone had been one of the leading architects of the historic pact with the attorneys general. He had been named CEO in October 1995, and he had believed it was in the best financial interests of his company to reach the settlement and reduce the legal liability facing the industry.

Now he was having second thoughts. On April 8, 1998, he had addressed the National Press Club in Washington and announced "that if [Congress] wanted to legislate his industry into oblivion, it could do so without his help."[35] It was a de facto declaration of war against the increasingly punitive proposals being heard in Congress. He later told a reporter, "I finally saw that there wasn't a chance in hell of any resolution to this problem in the near future."[36]

In reaching this decision, Goldstone was choosing to pursue a high-risk strategy of backing off the publicly negotiated settlement with the state attorneys general and of attempting to stop legislation that many already conceded was going to pass in some form. It was not clear that this approach was going to be effective.

But Goldstone had an ace up his sleeve. Unbeknownst to tobacco critics, he had authorized both a ground war and an air war. The former would emphasize lobbying and litigation. Goldstone warned his critics, "We will spend years in the courtroom, and we will do every possible thing to fight for our rights."[37] It was one thing to raise taxes, he felt. It was wholly another to impose advertising restrictions on his business, which were problematic because of the First Amendment. Goldstone believed he could win in the courts on that issue.

The air war featured a $40 million public advocacy campaign that would label the congressional proposal as a big tax increase. Using television and newspaper ads, the effort would attempt to do to the hopes for tobacco legislation what the "Harry and Louise" ads run by the Health Insurance Association of America had done to Clinton's hopes for health care reform.[38] The spots would help turn ordinary persons against Congress.

Deep down, Goldstone had great faith in his fellow citizens. "I am very confident that the American people are more willing to listen than the people in Washington are," he said.[39] With proper education, the members of the public would see the value of his argument.

Based on this assumption, the tobacco industry's commercials warned of "a flourishing, violent black market" that would result from a dramatic rise in the price of cigarettes. Prohibition had created an underground trade in liquor dominated by organized crime; Goldstone was playing on public fears that the same would happen with cigarettes. The ads also raised the dreaded "tax" issue, on the assumption that doubling of federal levies on cigarettes was a big tax increase of the sort the American people did not like.

By June 1998 the tobacco legislation was dead. Despite public interest in the crackdown, the Republican-controlled Senate was unable to pass the antismoking bill. In combination with generous campaign contributions to GOP politicians, the television ads had killed support for a bill everyone had expected to pass. It was a remarkable demonstration of the power of money to dictate the policy agenda of Congress.

Republicans immediately pledged to push for more-limited legislation. In the House, Speaker Newt Gingrich announced, "[O]ur goal is to reduce teen smoking, not increase taxes." In the Senate, Majority Leader Trent Lott said Congress had expanded the bill way too far. "We've lost sight of the original noble cause of just dealing with teen-age smoking and drug abuse," he indicated.[40]

Promising to make use of the defeat in the upcoming election, Clinton aides predicted that "many key swing voters will decide that Republicans killed the bill because they were beholden to the tobacco industry, perhaps the most unpopular lobby in Washington."[41] In the 1998 voting, however, Republicans retained control of both the House and Senate, although by a reduced margin in the House.

Conclusion

The battle over tobacco illustrates the political difficulties of beating a powerful opponent armed with money for campaign contributions and television advertisements. Tobacco had not been the first to demonstrate this point. Indeed, the industry's was only the last in a long line of victories where powerful special interests had beaten back a Congress determined to stand up for collective interests.

Like the victory of insurers and small business owners over Clinton's attempt at health care reform in 1994, the tobacco lobby had triumphed over Congress in 1998 in a situation few thought was winnable. Given the political and public mood, most believed the House and Senate would pass the historic legislation regulating tobacco.

Industry leaders had followed the pattern of past victorious campaigns. Their effort combined inside lobbying directed at Congress, greased with campaign contributions and soft-money donations, and outside lobbying directed at the American people. Such campaigns were expensive, in this case costing as much as $40 million. But this was cheap with the future of an entire industry at stake.

The victory confirmed the "investment theory" of politics. Expenditures for lobbying Congress and influencing the electorate usually yielded big dividends for the industry concerned. It was cheaper to spend money on politics and get unfavorable regulations amended, killed, or removed than it was to pay the cost of complying with the new law.[42] After years of contributions, philanthropy, and public relations work, big tobacco was able to withstand enormous political pressures, mobilize a base of "angry taxpayers" that it had in fact created, and cajole its legislative friends into stopping a bill that was seen as nearly unstoppable.

The defeat of the tobacco legislation marked just one more example of how money talks in Washington. In cases as disparate as the Teamsters, Archer Daniels Midland, Koch Industries, and tobacco, strong interests have gained disproportionate advantages from public officials in need of contributions. Big money continues its reign in American politics.

CHAPTER 8

Non-Profits, Foundations, and Tax-Exempt Organizations

I T   I S   L O C A T E D   in an antiques store in Wingate, North Carolina, far away from the scrutiny of the New York and Washington press corps. Affiliated with a small private school called Wingate College, the Jesse Helms Center was started in 1988 as a tax-exempt charitable foundation.

According to Internal Revenue Service filings, the organization has assets of more than $5 million and has raised hundreds of thousands of dollars from foreign governments, such as those of Taiwan ($225,000) and Kuwait ($100,000). R. J. Reynolds ($750,000), Philip Morris ($200,000), United States Tobacco ($100,000), and the textile magnate Roger Milliken ($225,000) are among other contributors.[1]

Its mission is to "maintain the records of U.S. Senator Jesse Helms" and "advance the principles and values important to good citizenship and to preserve our liberties as a free and moral people." Among its activities are a museum devoted to the life and writings of Senator Helms, a lecture series that has hosted Steve Forbes, Clarence Thomas, and Jeane Kirkpatrick, and an annual Free Enterprise Leadership conference for high school students.[2]

As a charitable foundation, the center is allowed to solicit tax-deductible gifts without releasing the names of donors. In return for this federal benefit, it is barred from engaging in political or electioneering activities. The organization is not required to disclose how it spends its money, other than reporting broad categories of expenditures on IRS tax forms.

Helms's staff at the center worked hard to maintain a legal separation between their own partisan political activities and its charitable work. A similar foundation organized earlier by Helms had seen its tax exemption revoked by the IRS because "it had participated in political activities and improperly benefited private individuals who were connected to conservative causes."[3] The senator and his friends did not want the Jesse Helms Center to suffer the same fate.

Yet troubling signs of political cooperation remained. According to press reports, there was substantial overlap between the center's board and Helm's political staff. For example, the executive director of the foundation, John Dodd, was a former fundraiser for the senator's re-election campaigns. Other board members included Helms's former chief legislative assistant, his current chief of staff from the Foreign Relations Committee, and two campaign treasurers. The center used the same mailing list as Helms's campaign.

If donors were contributing directly to the senator, federal election law would limit them to $1,000 in individual gifts or $5,000 in corporate contributions. As illustrated in Chapter 5, donations by foreign governments to federal candidates are clearly prohibited by law. This restriction was especially relevant for Helms, given his chairmanship of the Senate Foreign Relations Committee. The specter of Taiwan or Kuwait influencing U.S. policy through charitable contributions to a committee chairman troubled everyone familiar with the gifts.

In relying on the Jesse Helms Center to promote his career and political beliefs, the senator was participating in the vanguard of a new mechanism that allowed private interests to fund politicians. As subtle as the use of loopholes to nurture the explosive growth of issue advocacy and independent expenditures, the Helms effort was consistent with the use of non-profit organizations, charitable foundations, and tax-exempt groups as sources of funds by other public officials.

The secrecy with which such gifts could be made, the absence of any limit on their size, and the clear potential involved for conflicts of interest represented new challenges in national politics. The emergence of this sort of funding raised troubling issues for those worried about the health of American democracy.

Gingrich and GOPAC

Helms was not the only politician who saw non-profit organizations as vehicles for political advancement. Newt Gingrich, a conservative House member from Georgia, believed non-profits and foundations could help Republicans regain control of Congress. The fiery leader set about bending an organization known as GOPAC to his own purposes.

The former governor of Delaware, Pete Du Pont, had

founded GOPAC in 1979 as a traditional political action committee. Its mission was to recruit citizens into local politics and
raise money for sympathetic candidates. The group was not
taken over by Gingrich until he became general chairman in
1986. The Georgian brought new energy to GOPAC. He quickly
grasped its potential for recruiting candidates and educating the
public outside the normal process of political organizations.

Exploiting a provision in the law that allowed non-profit
groups to engage in public education without having to register
as political action committees, Gingrich turned GOPAC into an
aggressive fundraising, candidate recruitment, and public education entity. For example, in 1992 the group budgeted $3.5 mil-
lion in order to attract quality candidates for 170 House races.[4]
None of its donors was publicly identified or restricted in the
amount of money she or he could contribute.

As the chief architect of the strategy to take back Congress,
Gingrich made sure GOPAC amply funded his travels and
speaking engagements. Every month, the group mailed four
thousand audiotapes of his speeches to grassroots activists
around the country to inspire them to support the pursuit of
freedom and opportunity. These tapes, along with a book
Gingrich wrote, described how Republicans seeking office could
communicate with the people to best effect.[5] Every week,
GOPAC also mailed several thousand GOP candidates advice
on how to frame their discussion of issues that were in the news.

Gingrich believed the organization represented "the most
sophisticated, most comprehensive effort to create new ideas in
American politics that I know of in my lifetime."[6] Although ded-
icated to making the Georgian Speaker of the House one day, it

was not until 1992 that the group started filing official campaign reports with the Federal Election Commission disclosing its spending and contributors.

The following year, Gingrich developed a novel technique for engaging in public education. He started a college course entitled "Renewing American Civilization," sponsored by Kennesaw State College, that would be broadcast by satellite to 133 locations around the country. Costing $290,000 and financed mainly by GOPAC and other conservative supporters, the course was "designed to find ways to replace the welfare state in America." Taught on ten Saturday mornings beginning in September 1993, and featuring Gingrich and political experts such as Larry Sabato of the University of Virginia, the class's goal was "to create a shared doctrine for perhaps a quarter-million citizen activists."[7]

After protests by campus faculty, the course moved in 1994 and 1995 to Reinhardt College, also in Georgia, where it was broadcast nationally on cable television. The costs for satellite transmission were paid by a tax-exempt organization founded by Gingrich called the Progress and Freedom Foundation.

Irate over what they considered a blatant political use of a tax-exempt foundation, Democrats in the House filed ethics charges against their colleague. The complaint, which Gingrich, now Speaker, settled in 1996 by apologizing and paying a $300,000 fine, alleged that he had not obtained proper legal advice on the course and had filed "false information" with the House's ethics panel when he wrote them that GOPAC had not been involved. In reality, the group had initially financed the satellite broadcasts of the course.[8]

A follow-up investigation by the Internal Revenue Service that lasted three and one-half years cleared Gingrich's Progress and Freedom Foundation of any legal wrongdoing. After reviewing records subpoenaed in the case, the IRS concluded tax laws had not been violated. The ruling was based on several factors, among them the "non-partisan content of the course, the favorable mention in the curriculum of officeholders who were not Republicans and the fact that the colleges at which the course was taught were well established."[9]

At the same time, though, the IRS did not clear the Abraham Lincoln Opportunity Foundation, which shared the "same offices, directors, employees and telephone numbers as GOPAC."[10] Run by Gingrich as an adjunct to his political-fundraising empire, the foundation had gone out of business in 1994. Originally, it had been created to help inner-city youths do something with their lives. As the Georgian became more politically prominent, however, he had redirected its efforts toward political fundraising and used it to broadcast his speeches nationwide. Late in 1998, the IRS revoked the tax-exempt status of the Abraham Lincoln Opportunity Foundation for allowing itself "to be used for non-exempt purposes by GOPAC."[11] According to news accounts, "GOPAC had loaned ALOF $45,000 in 1990 and $29,500 in 1991. Charitable contributions raised by ALOF were used to repay GOPAC for these loans."[12]

The Idea Spreads

Seeing an opportunity for political advancement, a number of non-profit groups have become more active in various campaigns. Such organizations as Americans for Tax Reform, the Christian Coalition, Citizens for Reform, and Vote Now '96 have become deeply involved in recent elections, often in direct coordination with one of the major parties.

Overall, non-profit groups working with political parties in 1996 received more than $12.5 million from donors steered their way by party officials.[13] Much of this money was used to finance attack ads and voter mailings criticizing political opponents.

Americans for Tax Reform, a conservative antitax group, received $4.6 million from the Republican National Committee in 1996 to organize last-minute mailings and phone calls.[14] The National Right to Life Committee got $650,000 to attack Democrats on the abortion issue. A group called the American Defense Institute, which specialized in raising the GOP turnout, took in $500,000 from Philip Morris at the request of the RNC.

After receiving its RNC contribution, Americans for Tax Reform used the money to finance a direct mail campaign in 150 congressional districts to "warn seniors about Democrat Mediscare tactics." Letters attempted to "reassure voters that their Medicare benefits would be protected by Republicans."[15]

Democratic critics condemned this transfer as a circumvention of campaign finance rules. "The R.N.C. could not, by law, run these ads on behalf of these candidates," said Senator Carl Levin of Michigan. "So the R.N.C. transferred this money to this anti-tax group and it ran its ads for them. This is coordination and this is control."[16]

Americans for Tax Reform also got involved in a California referendum campaign on restricting unions in using membership dues for political activities. Taking advantage of its status as a tax-exempt educational group, ATR raised millions for this effort, as well as for another ballot proposal in support of no-fault auto insurance. In so doing, ATR sought to weaken two of the strongest allies of the Democrats, unions and trial lawyers, both big contributors to the party.[17]

Democrats played the same game, though. A Florida non-profit known as Vote Now '96, which worked to boost voter turnout in minority areas, had $3 million in large contributions steered to it by White House deputy chief of staff Harold Ickes. Often financed by individuals who could not contribute legally to the party or to Clinton, non-profits became a way of laundering money that might otherwise spark political controversies.[18] Indeed, at one White House dinner hosted by the president, donors were told they could contribute either to the Democratic party or, if they wanted anonymity, to Vote Now '96, which would ensure their money was used to help the campaign effort.[19]

The Democratic National Committee directed a $450,000 gift from an international businessman to Vote Now '96; $50,000 went from a Detroit leader to the National Coalition on Black Voter Participation in order to improve minority turnout.[20] Each donor had business contracts pending before federal agencies. Party officials justified the secrecy behind the political contributions as "a privacy matter" for donors who did not want to be identified publicly.[21]

Still more non-profit organizations aggressively entered the political realm. Although ostensibly a religious group, the Christian Coalition used voter guides to inform its supporters about the policy positions of candidates. Since it felt this activity fell within the area of public education, not partisan campaigning, the coalition did not register as a political action committee or comply with the Federal Election Commission's rules on disclosure of contributors and spending.

Worried about the political activism of the Christian Coalition, the FEC initiated an investigation that led to a lawsuit in 1996 about the group's activities in the 1992 presidential campaign. Focusing specifically on the public education enterprise, the FEC alleged that the voter guides represented "prohibited coordinated expenditures" and therefore violated federal campaign laws. These advisories were "made for no other reason than to influence an election" Steven Hershkowitz, an FEC lawyer, argued in court.[22]

In gathering evidence for this case, the FEC discovered frequent contacts between the Christian Coalition's executive director, Ralph Reed, and officials who worked at the Bush-Quayle campaign. Not only were there hundreds of phone calls back and forth, but Reed sat in on strategy sessions with Bush's advisors where plans to neutralize Ross Perot's support among religious voters were discussed. According to one written memo, Reed argued the voter guides would hurt the Reform party candidate "by revealing Perot's stance on certain social issues." According to court papers, Reed also helped President Bush's candidacy by giving him advance copies of questions that Pat Robertson would ask him during a *700 Club* television interview.[23]

Beyond the presidential level, a conservative non-profit organization known as Citizens for Reform devoted more than

$3 million in 1996 to attacking Democrats running for Congress. Senate investigators found that this money was provided to Citizens for Reform through Triad Management Service by the Koch family of Kansas and the Cone family of Pennsylvania, both large conservative donors. The gifts later were transferred to the non-profit outside political disclosure rules.

Had these contributions gone directly to the candidates, each individual donor would have been limited to $1,000 gifts and the contribution would have been publicly disclosed.[24] By working through non-profits, contributors are able to avoid gift limits and bypass public scrutiny of their electioneering activities.

Presidential Candidates' Foundations

Not to be outdone by interest groups, would-be presidents have jumped into the foundation dodge. In 1993, for example, Senator Bob Dole organized a tax-exempt group called the Better America Foundation, which he used to finance a million-dollar television campaign supporting a balanced budget.

Between the group's inception and its disbanding two years later, Dole raised $4.6 million from eighty-six companies and wealthy individuals. Nineteen donors gave at least $100,000 each. In 1995, however, when the foundation's secrecy grew controversial, Dole terminated the organization and offered to return gifts to donors.[25]

About the same time that Dole created his group, Lamar Alexander, the former governor of Tennessee, organized the Republican Exchange Satellite Network as a forum for his political views. It raised $4.5 million from 255 different contributors. Fourteen gave at least $100,000 and another 140 donated at least $10,000. Monthly newsletters were mailed to fifteen thousand GOP activists and the organization hosted nineteen "Neighborhood Meetings" led by Alexander. The group also financed a "drive across America" and a full-time organizer for the important caucus state of Iowa. Indicative of its real purpose, once Alexander announced officially for the presidency most of the staff transferred to the campaign operation.[26]

One of the biggest organizations set up as an outgrowth of political activities was American Cause, created by Pat Buchanan. Started in 1993 after his first failed try for the Republican presidential nomination, the non-profit group was run by his sister, Bay Buchanan, and used to pay for Pat's travel and speech making around the country. In its first year, the organization raised a million dollars to finance a television advertising campaign against the North American Free Trade Agreement and provide a forum for Pat Buchanan.[27]

Designed carefully to comply with federal tax rules, American Cause had both a tax-exempt education division and a tax-paying lobbying and politics group. One of the chief aims of the latter was to employ the advisors Buchanan had assembled for his 1992 run well before his 1996 campaign got under way.

Although there is no requirement that the identities of donors be disclosed, news accounts revealed that Roger Milliken, a South Carolina textile manufacturer, had given $1.8 million to American Cause. Milliken is a big donor to a variety of conservative causes and had previously been a major backer of Newt Gingrich's GOPAC.

Republicans were not the only ones to generate negative publicity through ties to foundations and charitable organizations. Vice President Al Gore earned months of unfavorable coverage for a fundraiser at the His Lai Buddhist temple, a tax-exempt religious organization. According to federal law, it is illegal to hold a political fundraiser in a church or temple. Initially, Gore pleaded ignorance about the meeting, claiming he thought it was a "community-outreach event." He later conceded, however, that this was in error. He had known the gathering was "finance related."[28]

Tax-Exempt Party Organizations

Political parties have gotten into the tax-exempt game as well. The Republican National Committee created something called the National Policy Forum, designed to be the "issue development subsidiary" of the GOP. Funded by "corporations, rich individuals and foreign donors," it raised several million dollars, including large sums from foreign sources.[29]

With its close ties to the RNC, it was difficult for party leaders to label the group a truly independent body pursuing the public interest. The forum had advisory boards featuring GOP legislators, state officials, and party operatives. These also were large numbers of financial transactions (such as loans and gifts) between the two organizations that generated suspicion among outside observers.

One critic, Don Simon of Common Cause, derided the National Policy Forum as "a mechanism to evade campaign finance laws."[30] Because non-profits and tax-exempt groups do

not have to disclose contributors or limit the amount of donations, they are an ideal vehicle for bypassing cumbersome federal campaign finance rules.[31]

The potential for conflicts of interest is rife with this kind of
organization. For example, in the middle of the congressional
deliberations on telecommunications reform in 1995, the National Policy Forum brought top industry leaders together with
the committee chairmen who were writing the legislation. The
executives later were approached for $25,000 contributions.[32]

However, shortly into its young life, the forum ran into trouble. For starters, the IRS denied its request for tax exemption on
the grounds that it was too closely aligned with the GOP. Then,
an investigation of questionable fundraising revealed that the
organization had received gifts and a $2.2 million loan guaran-
tee from Ambrose Tung Young, a Hong Kong businessman. The
forum returned $122,000, the first time the Republican party
ever had to give back a foreign contribution. Due to all these
difficulties, the group was permanently disbanded in 1996.[33]

The IRS Cracks Down

With the growing level of political activity going on under the
rubric of tax-exempt foundations, the IRS has started to get
much tougher in upholding requests for exempt status. With
more than 1.5 million tax-exempt organizations in the United
States, the IRS worried that groups were using the implicit government subsidy of tax exemption to pursue political and electoral objectives in violation of the federal tax code.[34]

One such organization targeted by the IRS was an abortion rights group that was active in Virginia and New Jersey during the 1989 gubernatorial races. Labeled the "Story of M" by the press since the name of the group was never released by the IRS, the episode illustrates the tough new attitude of tax code enforcers. According to court papers, this was the first case of the IRS revoking a tax exemption due to direct mail letters the agency found that crossed the line into electioneering.

Unlike the FEC, which faces the delicate task of trying to distinguish political from electoral activities, the IRS bans "all forms of participation or intervention in any political campaign."[35] Its reasoning is that even though the courts have upheld the importance of freedom of speech, there is no constitutionally guaranteed right to tax-subsidized expression. Tax-exempt groups have no legal grounds for using their privileged status for any partisan political activity.

Hence, when tax auditors found fundraising solicitations from the group in question that said, "[T]ogether, we can change the shape of American politics," they concluded that voter education was becoming voter direction. Even though the organization never used language expressing support of or opposition to a particular candidate, which is the hallmark of the FEC's express-advocacy standard, the IRS concluded the group had participated in electioneering by making "politically oriented statements to [its] intended audience."[36]

In another case, the IRS denied a tax exemption to the Fund for the Study of Economic Growth and Tax Reform after finding that it was too closely tied to the Republican party. Organized by GOP politician Jack Kemp, the group had an "all-Republican, 14-member commission" appointed by the party's congressional leaders, Newt Gingrich and Bob Dole.[37]

The decision, which was affirmed by a federal judge, has ramifications for traditional interpretations holding that official governmental bodies can request charitable groups to study issues without risking the tax-exempt status of those groups. However, in the judge's view "the Fund clearly supported a one-sided political agenda and did not operate exclusively for nonexempt purposes." Each of these features gave sufficient cause to deny the exemption.[38]

In a lawsuit against the United Cancer Council, a now defunct Indiana fundraising group, a federal appeals court ruled that the IRS cannot revoke an organization's tax exemption just because fundraisers kept most of the donations. The case involved a direct mail company that was used to help the UCC solicit funds for cancer prevention. After sending out eighty million letters, the mail operation raised $28.8 million; $2.3 million went to the charity. According to the judge, incompetent or foolish fundraising was not grounds for revoking a group's tax-exempt status.[39]

An organization called the Freedom Alliance, associated with Iran-Contra figure Oliver North, lost its exemption on two grounds. First, according to the tax agency, North violated rules against electioneering by attacking the policies of presidential aspirant Tom Harkin in 1991 during a nationally broadcast radio show. He claimed Harkin had a "failed" philosophy and was a "divisive figure."[40]

In addition, the IRS accused the organization of improperly

"providing financial or other types of benefits" to North, who ran it. After investigating, the IRS concluded he had "personally benefited from a campaign waged by the Freedom Alliance seeking to repeal the independent counsel law and cut off funds to Independent Counsel Lawrence Walsh."[41] This effort was thought to have helped North in his 1994 U.S. Senate race against Charles Robb, the incumbent, in Virginia. The group also funded North's radio show, a monthly newsletter featuring him, and periodic fundraising mailings on his behalf.

In 1999, a federal court upheld an IRS decision removing the tax exemption of the Church at Pierce Creek in New York. A few days before the 1992 presidential election, the church had taken out full-page ads in *USA Today* and the *Washington Times* condemning the Democratic nominee's policies on abortion, homosexuality, and sex education. Entitled "Christian Beware," the advertisements proclaimed that "Bill Clinton is promoting policies that are in rebellion to God's laws" and that Americans should not "put the economy ahead of the Ten Commandments." A line at the bottom informed readers, "[T]ax-deductible donations for this advertisement gladly accepted."[42]

After the IRS revoked its tax-exempt status in 1995, the church sued. But U.S. District Judge Paul L. Friedman ruled that the church had engaged in improper political activities in running ads critical of a presidential candidate right before the election. Groups that did not have to pay taxes could not engage in partisan political activity, he said.

Following these and other investigations into tax status abuses—mainly directed at conservative groups, which have tended to be the ones pushing the fundraising envelope—congressional leaders announced their intention to hold hearings on why the IRS "had singled out conservative tax-exempt organizations for audits."[43]

According to its critics, the IRS was much more aggressive in investigating conservative than liberal groups. Among the organizations that had been audited were Citizens against Government Waste, the Heritage Foundation, the National Rifle Association, Gingrich's Progress and Freedom Foundation, and North's Freedom Alliance, all of which supported conservative political agendas.[44]

As a sign of how contentious IRS decisions were becoming, Congressman Bill Archer of Texas, chairman of the House Ways and Means Committee, raised eyebrows when it was discovered that he personally had asked the commissioner of the IRS "to ensure fair treatment for the Christian Coalition's application for tax-exempt status."[45] For eight years, the group's application had been pending at the agency without any formal decision. In a private meeting with the commissioner, Archer had raised the subject and asked that the IRS decide the issue "in a fair and impartial manner."[46] In 1999, however, the Christian Coalition's request for a tax exemption was denied, and the group was split into political and non-political wings.[47]

This unusual political intrusion into the internal decisions of the tax agency drew immediate criticism from the Democratic National Committee. Condemning Archer, Chairman Roy Romer said, "[T]he Republican leadership has channeled its energies on advancing the agenda of right-wing organizations."[48]

Conclusion

After seeing the tremendous expansion in the political use of non-profits and tax-exempt groups, it is clear that they have become a major new tool for elected (and electing) officials. These organizations have several advantages over more traditional groups: contributions can be made secretly, there are no caps on the size of gifts, and there is no required disclosure of spending. In the case of tax-exempts, contributors furthermore can claim a deduction on income tax forms; depending on the tax status of the individual, this can amount to anywhere from 14 to nearly 40 percent of the donation.

In a political system that increasingly involves controversial groups or wealthy donors attempting to influence the making of policy, stealth electioneering undermines the ability of citizens to determine the sources of public education campaigns that are aimed at them.[49] Studies of advertising, for example, clearly show that the credibility of the messenger affects the degree to which the message is effective. Sources with high public credibility are much more likely to be believed than are those whose credibility is weak.

One of the biggest difficulties of the contemporary era is that, because of the reliance on non-profit groups and foundations that are not required to identify their contributors, the people cannot know who is behind major lobbying campaigns and electioneering activities. Until men and women have the information necessary to evaluate the messenger, they are in a weak position to assess the message.

Foundations are especially problematic as funding vehicles

because of their tax-exempt status. By relying on exempt organizations, politicians essentially receive a subsidy from the federal government for what in reality are clandestine political activities. It is one thing for those seeking election or re-election to use non-profits as a way to circumvent disclosure laws. But it is much more serious when such activities are made possible by a federal handout. A tax subsidy for partisan political activities amounts to direct government intervention on behalf of a favored party in the country's political process.

CHAPTER 9

Conclusion

FROM INDEPENDENT expenditures on the Willie Horton commercial and issue advocacy by the Christian Action Network to soliciting money from foreign nationals and using tax-exempt foundations for stealth electioneering, it is clear that the post-Watergate era campaign finance system has completely broken down. Checkbook democracy has emerged in its stead, with secrecy, large contributions, and unaccountable public officials. What used to represent a reasonably clear set of rules for the game now has given way to a bewildering variety of tangled laws, confusing regulations, blatant loopholes, and selective enforcement of what guidelines remain. It is a system that poses serious legal and political dangers to candidates and contributors alike.

Every new campaign brings headlines exploring the latest financial abuses. Millionaires donate hundreds of thousands of dollars to influence the election, as do unions, corporations, and special-interest groups. The president rents out the Lincoln Bedroom to big donors. Congressional candidates spend half their time raising funds instead of doing the people's business. Noncitizens give money to the political parties. Groups run ads about the candidates right before the voting without any required disclosure of their activities. Faced with complex rules, contributors are turned into white-collar criminals for violating laws they do not always understand.

Despite the stream of news stories documenting such questionable behavior, nothing seems to change. The citizenry does not see campaign finance reform as a political priority. In a striking rejoinder to the old line that crime does not pay, there have been few penalties for the systematic fundraising misdeeds that have taken place. The rules are so vague and so riddled with loopholes that convictions are rare. In the political arena, the voters do not punish parties or individual candidates who flout campaign finance laws.

Not surprisingly, political leaders do little to improve the process. By a two-to-one margin, the Senate refuses to propose a constitutional amendment that would allow limiting contributions and spending in federal elections. A reform package put forward by Senators John McCain (R-Ariz.) and Russell Feingold (D-Wis.) that would ban large, unregulated "soft money" contributions and restrict political action committees goes nowhere. A proposal to swap free television time for voluntary spending limits attracts only lukewarm support. Few politicians are in a hurry to make changes in our system of political finance.

This chapter discusses why, despite the fundamental importance of campaign finance abuses, little progress has been made. Political parties haven't seriously addressed improprieties in how campaigns are funded because they benefit from the current system. The courts have adopted a mistaken view that equates freedom of speech with the freedom to spend. Reporters help to inculcate in citizens a cynicism so massive that campaign finance scandals are seen as more of the same and confirmation that everyone breaks the law. Academics perpetuate the problem through studies suggesting money doesn't matter all that much in voting in the United States. Until these things change, it will remain very difficult to make American elections more open, fair, and equitable.

Why the Parties Won't Reform Campaign Finance

The Parties Like the Current System. Washington's dirty little secret about campaign finance is that the major players are happy with things as they are. Incumbents do very well under contemporary rules. In recent elections, more than 90 percent of the men and women who have sought re-election to Congress have won.

Why? Money. It's much easier for incumbents to raise campaign money than it is for challengers. Persons currently in office can provide access and influence legislation in ways impossible for those who aren't. Incumbents almost always have much higher name identification than challengers, and this biases the game against the dark horses before they have even begun to campaign.

In the past, politicians have changed financing rules only when the people have gotten so mad as to threaten the very legitimacy of the system. It takes the specter of serious public discontent for the parties to embrace meaningful reform. Otherwise, they will dilly and dally and talk about change, but do little to actually bring it about.

Around the turn of the nineteenth century, for example, citizens' anger over the depredations of the robber barons led to an outright ban on business contributions to candidates for federal office. Individuals could make donations, but corporations could not.[1] The idea was that companies held such superior financial resources that they put at risk the crucial democratic principles of fair and equitable electoral competition.

That limitation didn't last long, though. Corporations merely transferred funds to employees and made sure the money went to favored candidates. Soon, the economic clout of big business had again translated itself into political might.

In the 1940s, concern over the rising power of organized labor led to an extension of the ban on corporate money to unions. Workers could contribute individually, but not en masse. Again, the idea was the same as it had been fifty years earlier. Large, organized resources threatened the essence of democratic equality. Unions could not be allowed to make direct gifts to candidates.

Of course, that restriction didn't work very well either. Much like corporations, organized labor figured out ways around the law. Some unions provided in-kind benefits to candidates, whereas others set up separate funds to channel money into the political process.

In the 1970s, the Watergate scandal toppled a president and united the country behind fundamental change. Public fury over the abuses of that time created an impetus to reform that was the most concerted since the Progressive Era. Politicians feared that if they did not act they too would be swept out of office.[2]

The result was a virtual revolution in our system of campaign finance. Wealthy contributors were limited in how much they could give to candidates. A system of public matching funds was created. Tougher disclosure rules were put in place. A powerful new agency, the Federal Election Commission, was created.

For several years, the system operated pretty much as intended. Big money was forced out of politics. Disclosure became the norm and the expectation. A vigilant press ensured that candidates followed the rules as they were written. Persons running for office understood they had to respect electoral fair play.

Over time, however, continual changes of seemingly minor provisions weakened the system's foundations. Today, there are so many loopholes in campaign finance rules that creative candidates and contributors can do virtually as they please. Through independent expenditures and issue advocacy, wealthy interests can spend as much as they want. Using non-profits and tax-exempt organizations, donors can funnel money into the election process without any fear of disclosure. If funds start running low, appeals can be made to foreign nationals and international corporations having American subsidiaries. The high re-election rate of incumbents makes it hard for the parties to get very serious about changing the status quo.

The Parties Are Protected by Public Cynicism. The biggest thing that shields politicians of both major parties is massive public cynicism. Indeed, the most significant change in public opinion over the past forty years has been the dramatic growth of this attitude. Whereas three-quarters of Americans in the 1950s believed you could trust public officials to do what was right, three-quarters now feel you *can't* trust public officials.

Voters today believe all politicians cheat and that few can be trusted. Officials are widely thought to be out for themselves and not terribly interested in the public good. The quest for campaign dollars has trumped all else in American politics.

In a period when headlines almost weekly publicize the latest campaign finance scandals, the people have become so desensitized to allegations of financial misdeeds that they assume little can be done about the problem. The constant barrage of scandals and the continuing parade of negative headlines confirm the widespread view that something fundamental is wrong in the political system.

Ironically, this very cynicism shields the major parties from political fallout and gives them little incentive to clean up the fundraising process. After all, if everyone is guilty, then no one can be punished. As long as the people continue to believe that all politicians cheat, there will be few meaningful consequences from the specific abuses that are uncovered.

The Major Parties Have Different Electoral Self-Interests. Although both Republicans and Democrats give lip service to the need to reform campaign finance, their behavior is another story. The main reason the parties cannot agree on reforming the system is that each has a different conception of its electoral self-interest.

Republicans are more likely to want to rid the system of political action committees and labor money, which generally help their opponents. Democrats are more likely to talk about outlawing soft-money contributions by millionaires and corporations, since the ultrarich tend to give to the GOP. Conservatives favor a disclosure-based system with few regulations on the assumption that they can out-raise liberals. For their part, liberals want to squeeze private contributions out of the political system and move toward public financing because they have more confidence in government-provided funds than in money from private sources.[3]

In this situation, it is easy for every faction to work to retain its particular fundraising advantage while piously complaining about the excesses of its opponents. Political groups can rest assured that each will veto the other's reforms and there will be no fundamental change in the financial status quo. For established players with lots of resources, it is a pretty good system.

Why the Courts Mistakenly Have Equated Freedom of Speech with Freedom to Spend

In its historic ruling in *Buckley v. Valeo,* the Supreme Court equated political spending with freedom of expression. Giving paid campaign speech a constitutional status equivalent to that of free speech has made it virtually impossible to regulate blatant abuses without trampling on what the Court considers constitutionally protected rights.

Since 1976, judicial decisions have redrawn the line between reportable electioneering and undisclosed "freedom of speech" activities to the point where more and more campaign-oriented efforts fall outside the sphere of public disclosure. Creative politicians and interest groups have exploited these new freedoms in ways that have moved the political system away from the very principles of openness, fairness, and equality of electoral competition emphasized in the reforms that followed Watergate.

The result has been a structure marred by significant gaps in disclosure rules, selective enforcement, the toleration of big contributions from privileged elements within society, and an electoral process that fundamentally favors incumbents over challengers. The explosion of such money loopholes as independent expenditures, issue advocacy, and tax-exempt foundations shifts American democracy back toward a state of affairs that many reformers decried nearly three decades ago.

What many forget about Watergate is that fundraising abuses made it possible for the Nixon White House to finance a systematic plan to disrupt opposition candidates. Many remember the president's obstruction of justice and abuse of office, but fail to note how much the overall scandal was driven by large, secret contributions from wealthy donors. The Supreme Court's reasoning in favor of disclosure rules, contributor limits, and voluntary equal spending caps in the presidential elections was based in large measure on the importance of avoiding either the reality or the perception of corruption in government.

The sad irony is that subsequent court judgments have lost sight of these historic principles in their rush to elevate one good, freedom of expression, over every other virtue. Large interests today can give unlimited amounts of money to influence the political process, either in the form of soft-money contributions to the parties, independent expenditures on behalf of a specific candidate, or issue advocacy through a non-profit interest group or a tax-exempt foundation.

Secrecy has become the hallmark of our emerging system.

Direct contributions to candidates or the parties must be disclosed publicly. But issue advocacy does not, and gifts in support of clandestine political activities that are funneled through nonprofits or foundations do not, have to be made public. It is a schizophrenic demarcation that fuels massive cynicism among all involved, from reporters and politicians to donors and the general public.

Until the courts recognize the need to balance freedom of expression with the equally important principles of openness, fairness, and equitable electoral competition, there can be no meaningful reform. It is one thing to respect the First Amendment, but completely another to place it in a supreme position over other cherished values. Indeed, the beauty of the 1970s' legislation was the careful manner in which it balanced competing constitutional and political principles.

Few would argue against the idea that freedom of expression is crucial to American democracy. The country has a long history of protected liberty in part due to this important constitutional safeguard. The multitude of voices freely speaking out on major issues is one of the things that makes our political system unique.

At the same time that freedom of expression is crucial, though, openness, fairness, and equity are equally important. Unless each side can agree on what the rules of the game are, and unless different interests have an equitable opportunity to make their views known in electoral discourse, the country will suffer.

At a minimum, democratic principles require public access to information about who is funding modern campaigns, what amounts of money are being spent to influence elections, and what types of organizations are allowed to engage in political activities.

With the full complicity of the courts, however, each of these basic principles has been seriously eroded. Politicians are freed of any legal obligation to respect rules of fair play. Each side is locked in a competitive battle to win tightly fought races. There is no incentive to be cautious in fundraising. Every loophole, every gray area must be exploited for partisan political advantage—if one side doesn't do it, the opposition will. Moderation in fundraising may cost you or your party victory in the next election.

It is the job of the courts to protect the integrity of the rules of the game. Right now, politicians are trapped in a "prisoners' dilemma" that encourages each side constantly to escalate its fundraising efforts. It is a race no one can win. There is no way the parties can stop this spiral as long as each believes the other is going to exploit loopholes. To play the game any other way is to risk electoral annihilation in the next campaign. If candidates cannot trust the opposition to stay within the bounds of commonly accepted behavior, a crucial tenet of democratic government is undermined. Without trust by the leadership in the principle that everyone plays by the same rules, the whole system risks a fundamental breakdown.

How the Media Perpetuate Citizens' Cynicism

It is not just parties and courts that aggravate the problems of money in politics. News reporting contributes to these difficulties because of the lack of proportionality in coverage and a tendency to develop every story from the theme that all politicians skirt the law. The need to "produce news" every day, no matter what has happened, provides an incentive to sensationalize even the smallest kind of campaign violation.

If anything, the rise of twenty-four-hour news networks and the fragmentation of the media marketplace exacerbate this problem.[4] The competitiveness of contemporary reporting pushes all journalists toward tabloid coverage. Few have incentives to underplay their stories. Everything becomes a scandal, from the mundane to the truly important.

The reality, of course, is that some fundraising violations are more serious than others and not all politicians break the law. The inability to educate the people about this reality presents a serious challenge to campaign finance reform and compromises the integrity of the entire democratic system.

With a citizenry that is very skeptical about everything related to the political process, journalists must understand that news coverage has to display a sense of proportionality. The candidate who accepts a $50 dinner from the lobbyist is not the same as a politician who follows a systematic plan to secretly raise millions in undisclosed gifts coordinated with non-profits, foundations, and tax-exempt organizations. The former may involve graft; the latter involves a system-wide threat that needs to be dissected so as to reveal how it is going to affect the political process.

Some activities go to the heart of the workings of democracy and competitive elections, whereas others are merely superficial violations of the law. Journalists must learn to distinguish fundamental problems involving campaign finance from trivial ones. Not only must they follow rules of proportionality, they must pose basic questions about the money trail. Where is the money coming from? How is it being spent? How does it influence the political process?

The creative ways campaign staffers discover to play the financing game means journalists must stay vigilant about new techniques for hiding fundraising. Just because candidates file timely finance reports does not mean that the documents contain all that is worth noting about political fundraising.

Too often, journalists are so interested in the game itself, with its questions of strategy and of who is winning and who is losing, that they give short shrift to the important policy stakes of campaign finance. The increasingly technical nature of the rules, the difficulties of ferreting out answers from creative political operatives, and the problems of interesting citizens in stories about how campaigns are financed make the job of the reporter very challenging.

Unless journalists figure out a way to follow the money trail in an era of stealth politics, they will fail in their historic mission of exercising political oversight in the United States. No other group has the institutional position or the public credibility to police this area of political conduct. If reporters do not do the job, no one else can pick up the slack.

How Academic Studies Undermine Reform

Scholarly investigators compound the problem of campaign finance reform by turning out studies suggesting that money is not really very important in American policymaking or national elections. For example, the interest group scholar John Wright concludes that campaign donations yield little fruit for congressional lobbyists: "Contributions and other material gifts or favors are not the primary sources of interest group influence in the legislative process."[5]

To his mind, information exchanges are more crucial than money per se. Information greases the skids between legislators and lobbyists because each needs new material in order to complete his or her job. Campaign contributions pale by comparison, he reasons.

The same logic appears in electoral studies. The political scientist Gary Jacobson claims that campaign spending is not a crucial factor in election outcomes. So long as challengers have sufficient money to be taken seriously and are able to communicate with the people, the person spending the most money has no guarantee of winning.[6]

These authors are not alone in their thinking. A surprisingly large number of research projects points to factors other than money as being at the heart of decision making. For example, such elements as party identification, issue beliefs, cultural values, media advertising, or group endorsements are often cited as crucial determinants of why things happen the way they do in America.

To the extent that each of these elements is important, it still does not outweigh the role that money plays. Cash can be important in all sorts of subtle and not-so-subtle ways. How women and men see political controversies can be influenced by how such things are framed and communicated to the people.

Groups can underwrite polls in order to show particular results. Well-produced advertisements can shift public impressions of current events. The timely release of research studies financed by special interests can tilt the public dialogue in one direction or another. In short, perceptions about political events are subject to manipulation.

What researchers need to remember is that money is a major factor shaping how persons see issues. Funding frames subjects, helps to communicate particular points of view to the general public, and leads to heightened awareness of specific ideological positions. It is best not to ignore the money trail below the surface of political events.

Common Approaches to Reform

In a situation in which the likelihood of fundamental change through legislative action is low because of how the political parties, courts, journalists, and academics impede reform, those interested in finding a new direction need to follow multiple paths. No one tactic by itself is going to be effective. Instead, it will take a variety of actions to move the country closer to open, fair, and equitable campaign finance.[7]

However, not all such actions that have been publicly proposed are going to work. Examining three common approaches to changing campaign finance, for example, reveals several problems that their advocates ignore.

1. Squeezing Private Money Out of Politics. This, the most popular strategy among reformers, involves attempting to limit how much candidates, political parties, and outside interest groups can spend.

The general idea behind this approach is that money is corrupting and that too much of it flowing around the political system raises conflicts of interest and exposes public officials to financial pressures. Given these fears, reformers support spending limits. In their eyes, the appropriate remedy is not more money, but less. Large contributors should be barred. Interest groups should not be allowed to broadcast ads at election time. Parties should face limits on soft-money contributions and independent expenditures. In general, anything that wrings private funds out of the process enhances the purity of the system and the ability of officials to conduct the people's business in a fair and just manner.

An example of this way of thinking can be found in California, where a businessman is sponsoring a ballot measure that would establish voluntary spending limits in gubernatorial races, raise contribution limits to $5,000 per election stage, forbid fundraising except in the year before a primary, and require large contributions to be disclosed over the World Wide Web within twenty-four hours of receipt.[8]

However, this approach is naive at best and dangerous at worst. The problem in American politics is not too much money; it is the availability and use of secret, undisclosed financial resources. In an era when large corporations spend huge amounts on advertising (IBM, for example, devotes $500 million annually to promoting its products), it makes little sense to limit the ability of politicians or groups to engage in public education. If anything, educational efforts are at the heart of democracy, as long as they are fully disclosed and accountable to the general public.

2. Subsidizing Electioneering. Another suggestion is to reward candidates who accept limits by giving them public money or free television time. Here, the emphasis is on positive inducements toward good behavior, not punishment for bad action.

For example, some have proposed that persons seeking office who agree to voluntarily cap their spending receive limited forms of public funding, such as the matching of small contributions below $250. This bypasses the problem courts have had with spending limits by imposing the condition only for candidates who opt in to the system.

Alternatively, others have suggested that candidates who cap their spending get free television time for direct appeals to the people. This allows them to run their campaigns and reach voters while also agreeing to spending limits.

These proposals show real promise if implemented. However, neither politicians nor broadcasters have shown much inclination to consider either one. We have public financing of presidential elections and some gubernatorial races, but there is little chance of Congress moving toward public financing of House or Senate campaigns. In addition, our nation's broadcasters fervently oppose most efforts to mandate free television time for political candidates. In their eyes, this is taking hours of extremely valuable broadcast time that belongs to them.

3. Improving Disclosure and Raising Limits. A third strategy takes a pragmatic approach. Rather than squeezing money out of the system or subsidizing electioneering, reformers in this camp feel it would be better to improve disclosure and raise contributor limits so that candidates can compete on a more equal footing with political parties and interest groups.

The underlying assumption is that the courts are never going to place limits on freedom of expression and that they will continue to equate spending with speech. As long as these sentiments do not change, there is no constitutional argument either for spending restrictions or for limits on issue advocacy or independent expenditures.

The best reformers can hope for is improved disclosure, higher contributor limits, and redefining issue advocacy so as to regulate electoral promotion that uses a candidate's name and likeness in the two months leading up to an election. Contributor limits should be increased beyond their 1970s' levels so that candidates have an easier time raising money from individuals and are not so dependent on special-interest groups.

A measure proposed by two Republican senators, Olympia Snowe of Maine and James Jeffords of Vermont, falls within the spirit of this reform. According to their legislation, contributor limits should be raised and indexed to inflation. Disclosure requirements also should be strengthened. For example, in an effort to address media-based issue advocacy, interest groups using the name or likeness of a candidate "that spend more than $10,000 on radio or TV ads at election time [would be required] to report donations of $500 or more to the FEC."[9] The bill defines "election time" as the two months preceding any vote.

This legislation is a step in the right direction, but it does not go far enough to remedy current campaign finance abuses.

If anything, it is too pragmatic to achieve the goals reformers should desire. For example, the proposal does not address such forms of political activity as direct mail, phone calls, or issue advocacy over the Internet. Each of these is becoming more important in electioneering, sometimes involving particularly egregious and misleading types of campaign appeals.

In addition, as a national bill the Snowe-Jeffords legislation is relevant only for state races involving candidates, not for initiatives and referenda. Unfortunately, these sorts of ballot issues are where special-interest groups are very active in articulating points of view and are oftentimes very influential with the people. Legislation needs to ensure that voters know who is financing public education efforts in all kinds of elections, not just those where candidates are involved.

Thirteen Steps to Campaign Finance Reform

In order to avoid the problems of other approaches, I outline here some specific measures that need to be undertaken to confront campaign finance abuses. Each of these addresses specific issues in financing campaigns and is designed to move the country further along the path to open, fair, and equitable elections.

1. Require On-Line Weekly Disclosure Reports. Right now, candidates and political parties are required to file quarterly accounts of their fundraising. This interval is not frequent enough to inform voters who the contributors are and where the money is being spent. Weekly, on-line statements will give the people financial information in a timely manner. In the age of the Internet, there is no reason citizens should not have quick, regular, and easy access to campaign finance filings.

2. Extend Disclosure Rules to Interest Groups for Campaign-Related Activities Right before Elections. In 1998, interest groups spent more than a quarter of a billion dollars outside the required disclosure process. They were able to avoid disclosure by labeling their campaign activities "public education," rather than "express advocacy" in support of or opposition to particular candidates.

Yet in focus groups considering ads aired about candidates two weeks before the election, the public could not see a difference between those that aimed to educate citizens and those that sought to influence the voting. Indeed, a Brown University national survey showed that 74 percent of Americans believe interest groups should be subject to the same campaign disclosure rules as candidates for office.

If interest groups want to contest American elections, they clearly have the right to do so. But they should participate within the framework of rules governing the election process. The greatest influx of money into politics has involved issue advocacy advertisements by interest groups and political parties. Nearly 40 percent of all ads in recent elections have been sponsored by persons other than those seeking office.

All ads that are about the candidates or are directed at their policy positions or personal views that appear in the sixty days before an election should be subject to the same disclosure rules as commercials broadcast by candidates (the approach suggested in the Snowe-Jeffords bill). Information on contributions supporting such commercials and expenditures made to broadcast them should be made available to the general public and journalists through mandatory filings with the Federal Election Commission.

The same should hold true for other campaign-related activities, such as direct mail, phone banks, and Internet advocacy. Each of these is becoming more prevalent and therefore needs to be addressed by reform legislation.

3. Raise Contributor Limits. Current ceilings that restrict contributions from individuals to $1,000 and contributions from political action committees to $5,000 have not been increased in more than twenty years. These levels should be indexed to inflation and raised periodically to reflect changing price levels.

For example, the amount equivalent to $1,000 in 1976 is about $2,500 today. The PAC contribution limit could be increased to $10,000. Raising the amounts women and men could contribute would help challengers compete more effectively with incumbents. Anything that helps candidates raise money directly puts them on a more level footing against opponents backed by the myriad interest groups, political parties, and wealthy individuals who finance political activities.[10]

4. Ban Soft Money. The most inequitable feature of contemporary campaign finance rules is the ability of millionaires and wealthy organizations to make unlimited donations to political parties. Banning these soft-money contributions would shield both business and labor groups from exorbitant fundraising appeals by the parties and revive a more egalitarian tradition in American elections.

Since much of this money no longer is being used for general party building but instead is going for attack ads in individual races, the original rationale for this exception no longer applies. Building parties is an important task, but soft money is now being used for electioneering.

5. Require Candidates to Register Political Action Committees in States Where They Live. Governor George Pataki recently exposed a new loophole in campaign finance rules when he registered his political action committee, 21st Century Freedom, in Virginia rather than New York. The reason, according to press reports, was "Virginia's lenient campaign finance laws [that] set no ceiling on business donations and require disclosure just twice this year."[11] If candidates and public officials are allowed to shop from state to state in search of the weakest disclosure rules, it will make a complete mockery of the few laws that remain in the current system. The practice should be banned immediately.

6. Encourage Debates and Forums. Incumbents have extraordinary advantages over challengers. Debates and forums where candidates present their ideas side by side, without having them filtered by reporters, improve campaign discourse and give voters a direct way to compare political contenders. Debates are one of the most popular and widely viewed features of any race. Unlike many political events, voters actually watch them and discuss the results with their family and friends.

In addition, debates and forums offer the highest degree of substantive information of any political event.[12] They certainly have more content than ads or news sound-bites, which are too short to convey anything of substance.

7. Strengthen Ad Sponsorship Rules. The text identifying the sponsor of televised campaign ads, often literally in fine print, now is on the screen for only five seconds, not long enough for many viewers to read it. Sponsors should be required to keep their identification line visible for the duration of the ad.

They also should use disclosure names that make sense to ordinary persons. Hiding behind nebulous organization names like Citizens for Reform tells voters nothing about the messenger. It matters who pays for ads and is behind the political activity they urge. These two changes would help voters hold sponsors accountable for messages that appear in political spots and would improve the accountability of the political process.

8. Create a Standard of Proportionality in Media Stories about Campaign Finance. The biggest problem journalists have in covering campaign finance stories is a lack of proportionality about wrongdoing. Typically, little distinction is made between minor, technical violations and systematic plans to eviscerate the political process. Reporters need to make such distinctions. So long as voters believe that everyone is breaking the law, they will not punish anyone for fundraising excesses.

9. Encourage the Mass Media to Discuss Reforms when Publicizing Abuses. Journalists play a valuable role in bringing political misdeeds to light, but they also have a responsibility to examine reform proposals that address those abuses. Linking violations to possible solutions would help voters focus on actions that would ameliorate future problems.[13] Reporters can educate citizens not just about various difficulties, but about the range of proposals that have been developed to deal with them.

10. Don't Forget Initiatives and Referenda. Much of the campaign finance debate focuses on candidate elections to the virtual exclusion of ballot issues. This ignores how large contributors and secret expenditures can structure policy discussions on questions to be decided by popular vote. Many of the abuses that would take place in candidate contests are doubly problematic in policy referenda.

11. Tighten Contribution Rules on International Corporations. With the rising tide of mergers and acquisitions around the world, it is inevitable that more foreign money is likely to flow into American campaigns. Although current rules require that overseas companies only donate funds earned from American subsidiaries, lax banking practices in many parts of the world make it virtually impossible to police this area of fundraising. Both reporters and regulators must be vigilant about an explosion of foreign money taking over our elections.

12. Restructure the Federal Election Commission. When it was created in 1974, the FEC was a powerful independent body with the authority to police election activities; it had ample resources and took its job very seriously. However, in recent years, congressional meddling has weakened the agency to the point where it no longer takes decisive action. Owing in part to budget and staff cuts, it takes years to investigate complaints. This is patently unfair to both the person making the allegation and the public official charged with a violation.

Even when the agency finds evidence of misconduct, the fines are paltry. Several election cycles often go by before complaints are resolved. The commission needs stronger weapons to enforce the law. Unless the FEC has sufficient staffing and resources, it cannot do the job required of it by law.

One possible change is to overhaul the agency's structure. Right now, there are six commissioners who oversee operations and make decisions on enforcement. The seats are divided evenly between Republicans and Democrats, and controversial moves often result in a deadlock along partisan lines. Such was the case during the investigation into the independent expenditure for the Willie Horton ad in 1988.

Given the high proportion of political independents among the electorate at large (40 percent in recent years), it is time to end the FEC's partisan format. Either commissioners should be chosen on a nonpartisan basis or, as in the case of the Food and Drug Administration, a single head of the agency should be appointed. This would help the commission take more effective actions against blatant fundraising abuses.

13. Support the IRS Crackdown on Tax-Exempt Groups Engaging in Partisan Political Activities. One of the hallmarks of our era has been the use of tax-exempt foundations and groups for political purposes. From Gingrich's and North's employment of such organizations to foundations created by national parties and presidential candidates, tax-subsidized activism has become the latest tool for political advancement. Both the IRS and the courts need to sharply limit this activity. There is no constitutional right to taxpayer-financed freedom of speech. As courts have ruled recently, groups can either be tax exempt or engage in politics, but not both. They have to choose their most important mission.

Conclusion

The current rules on campaign finance need fundamental overhaul. Future reform should focus on better disclosure, raising contributor limits, regulating tax-exempt political activism, placing more "issue advocacy" under the rubric of electioneering, and ensuring that international mergers and acquisitions do not turn the funding of American candidates over to foreign nationals.

Today, nearly half of the money spent on elections falls outside required public disclosure. The American taxpayer provides some of it as a de facto subsidy through tax-exempt organizations. Other funds come from governments and corporations overseas. This torrent of secret money confirms citizens' cynicism, contributes to the negative spirit of election campaigns because of its fundamental unaccountability, and puts contributors at grave risk of selective enforcement action at the behest of political enemies bent on revenge.

If voters are to hold elected officials accountable, they need to know who is financing American campaigns, how much is being given, and what the money is being used for. That was the heart of the 1970s' legislation on campaign finance. Until we restore basic democratic principles to electoral competition in the United States, Americans will continue to be befuddled, angered, and ill served by our political process.

Notes

CHAPTER I

1. R. W. Apple, Jr., "Campaign Funds at Center of Wisconsin Race," *New York Times,* October 23, 1998, p. A1.
2. Helen Dewar, "Senate Kills Campaign Finance Bill," *Washington Post,* June 26, 1996, p. A4.
3. Crocker Stephenson and Meg Jones, "Thompson, Feingold Hold Big Election Leads, Poll Shows," *Milwaukee Journal Sentinel,* August 10, 1998, p. 1.
4. Apple, "Campaign Funds," p. A1.
5. Alan Borsuk, "Democratic Party Ad to Run Despite Feingold's Protests," *Milwaukee Journal Sentinel,* October 24, 1998, p. 11.
6. Lawrence Sussman, "Ads Decry Feingold's Vote on Interstate Abortion Bill," *Milwaukee Journal Sentinel,* November 1, 1998, p. 3.
7. Eric Pianin, Ben White, and Bill McAllister, "Ads Turn Nasty in Wisconsin Senate Bid," *Washington Post,* October 4, 1998, p. A21.
8. Borsuk, "Democratic Party Ad to Run," p. 11.
9. Richard Dunham, "Campaign-Finance Reform: Can Business Break the Logjam?" *Business Week,* April 5, 1999, p. 49.
10. Darrell M. West and Burdett A. Loomis, *The Sound of Money: How Political Interests Get What They Want* (New York: W. W. Norton, 1998), p. 46.
11. E. Joshua Rosenkranz, ed., *If "Buckley" Fell* (New York: Century Foundation, forthcoming, 1999); Anthony Corrado, Thomas Mann, Daniel Ortiz, Trevor Potter, and Frank Sorauf, *Campaign Finance Reform: A Sourcebook* (Washington, D.C.: Brookings

Institution Press, 1998); and Michael Malbin and Thomas Gais, *The Day after Reform* (Albany, N.Y.: Rockefeller Institute Press, 1998).

CHAPTER 2

1. Darrell M. West, *Air Wars: Television Advertising in Election Campaigns, 1952–1992* (Washington, D.C.: Congressional Quarterly Press, 1993), chapter 1.
2. "How Bush Won," *Newsweek,* November 21, 1988, p. 117.
3. For a discussion of these changes, see Herbert Alexander, *Financing Politics,* 2nd ed. (Washington, D.C.: Congressional Quarterly Press, 1980).
4. See Case 424 U.S. 1, 47–48, 58–59 (1976).
5. West, *Air Wars.*
6. Martin Schram, "The Making of Willie Horton," *New Republic,* May 28, 1990, p. 17.
7. Donald Kinder and Lynn Saunders, *Divided by Color* (Chicago: University of Chicago Press, 1996), p. 235.
8. Kathleen Hall Jamieson, *Dirty Politics* (New York: Oxford University Press, 1992), pp. 17–23.
9. West, *Air Wars,* pp. 141–143.
10. Ibid., p. 120.
11. Ibid., p. 112.
12. Marjorie Hershey, "The Campaign and the Media," in *The Election of 1988,* ed. Gerald M. Pomper (Chatham, N.J.: Chatham House, 1989), pp. 95–96.
13. Tali Mendelberg, "Executing Hortons: Racial Crime in the 1988 Presidential Campaign," *Public Opinion Quarterly,* Volume 61, 1997, p. 151.
14. August 1, 1990, Larry McCarthy Affidavit filed before the Federal Election Commission, Certified Administrative Record in Matter Under Review 3069, August 4, 1992, Volume 1, p. 60.
15. Ibid., p. 62.

16. August 1, 1990, Roger Ailes Affidavit filed before the Federal Election Commission, Certified Administrative Record in Matter Under Review 3069, August 4, 1992, Volume 1, p. 230. Also see August 29, 1991, Roger Ailes Deposition, MUR 3069, August 4, 1992, Volume 2, p. 531.

17. Ibid.

18. See U.S. District Court for the District of Columbia case, *Eugene Branstool, James M. Ruvolo, Ohio Democratic Party, William L. Mallory, Ray Miller, and Black Elected Democrats of Ohio v. Federal Election Commission,* C.A. No. 92-0284 (WBB), filed April 4, 1995, pp. 4–5.

19. Ibid., p. 10.

20. Ibid., p. 14.

21. Eliza Newlin Carney, "Party Time," *National Journal,* October 19, 1996, pp. 2214–2218. Also see Michael Malbin and Thomas Gais, *The Day after Reform* (Albany, N.Y.: Rockefeller Institute Press, 1998), p. 130.

22. Paul Hendrie, "Sneak Attacks: Issue Ads Evade Limits," *Capital Eye* (Washington, D.C.: Center for Responsive Politics), December 1998, p. 5.

23. Carney, "Party Time," pp. 2214–2218.

24. Hendrie, "Sneak Attacks," p. 5.

CHAPTER 3

1. *Buckley v. Valeo,* 424 U.S. 1 (1976), see note 52.

2. Eliza Newlin Carney, "Air Strikes," *National Journal,* June 15, 1996, pp. 1313–1317, and Peter Stone, "Business Strikes Back," *National Journal,* October 25, 1997, pp. 2130–2133.

3. See Martin Mawyer, "Dole's Lost Army of Christian Soldiers," *Washington Post,* October 13, 1996, p. C4, and Martin Mawyer, "Same-Sex Marriage Is Oxymoronic," *Providence Journal,* January 10, 1996, p. B6.

4. See *FEC v. Christian Action Network, Inc.,* Civil Action No. 94-0082-L, 894 F. Supp. 946, 952 (W.D. Va. 1995).

5. Darrell M. West, "An Analysis of Ads Run by the Christian Action Network, Inc., in 1992," February 6, 1995, unpublished paper.

6. Darrell M. West, *Air Wars: Television Advertising in Election Campaigns, 1952-1996,* 2nd ed. (Washington, D.C.: Congressional Quarterly Press, 1997).

7. James C. Turk Memorandum Opinion in *FEC v. Christian Action Network, Inc.,* Civil Action No. 94-0082-L, p. 2.

8. Ibid., p. 23.

9. Carney, "Air Strikes," pp. 1313-1317.

10. Ibid.

11. Ibid.

12. Deborah Beck, Paul Taylor, Jeffrey Stanger, and Douglas Rivlin, "Issue Advocacy during the 1996 Campaign," report by the Annenberg Public Policy Center of the University of Pennsylvania, September 16, 1997.

13. Darrell M. West and Burdett A. Loomis, *The Sound of Money: How Political Interests Get What They Want* (New York: W. W. Norton, 1998).

14. West, *Air Wars,* 2nd ed., p. 169.

15. Annenberg Public Policy Center report, "Issue Advocacy Advertising during the 1997-1998 Election Cycle," December 1, 1998.

16. Paul Hendrie, "Sneak Attacks: Issue Ads Evade Limits," *Capital Eye* (Washington, D.C.: Center for Responsive Politics), December 1998, p. 5.

17. Ibid.

18. Stone, "Business Strikes Back," pp. 2130-2133, and Peter Stone, "Lobbying and Law," *National Journal,* July 20, 1998.

19. Alliance for Better Campaigns, "Party Issue Ads Become Weapon of First Resort, Study Finds," *Political Standard,* December 1998-January 1999, p. 3.

20. West and Loomis, *The Sound of Money.*

21. E. E. Schattschneider, *The Semi-Sovereign People* (New York: Holt, Rinehart, and Winston, 1960).

CHAPTER 4

1. Herbert Alexander, *Financing Politics,* 4th ed. (Washington, D.C.: Congressional Quarterly Press, 1992), p. 12.
2. Francis Russell, *The Shadow of Blooming Grove: Warren G. Harding in His Times* (New York: McGraw-Hill, 1968).
3. Robert Caro, *The Years of Lyndon Johnson,* vol. 2, *Means of Ascent* (New York: Alfred A. Knopf, 1990).
4. Alexander, *Financing Politics,* p. 21. Also see David Adamany and George Agree, *Political Money* (Baltimore: Johns Hopkins University Press, 1975).
5. Alexander, *Financing Politics,* p. 18. Also for a history of campaign finance, see Frank Sorauf, *Inside Campaign Finance* (New Haven, Conn.: Yale University Press, 1992).
6. Michael Goodwin, "Steinbrenner and 'Star Quality,' " *New York Times,* August 23, 1987, sec. 5, p. 1.
7. Manny Topol, "George's Pardon Criticized," *Newsday,* February 5, 1989, p. 18, and *Chicago Tribune,* "Reagan Pardons Yanks' Boss," January 20, 1989, p. C14.
8. Alexander, *Financing Politics,* p. 20.
9. Joe Stephens, "Pool-Toy Entrepreneur Has History of Fund-Raising for GOP," *Kansas City Star,* April 21, 1996, p. 1, and Anthony Flint, "Through Politics, Fireman Sought Identity," *Boston Globe,* July 22, 1996, p. A1.
10. Associated Press Newswire, "Mass. Company Made Payoffs for Dole Contributions," April 21, 1996.
11. American Political Network Hotline, "Dole: Wants Investigation of Illegal-Contribution Charge," April 22, 1996.
12. Ibid., and Stephens, "Pool-Toy Entrepreneur," p. 1.
13. Fox Butterfield, "Ex-Aide to Dole Campaign Admits Illegal Contributions," *New York Times,* July 11, 1996, p. B10, and Joe Stephens, "Ex-Dole Aide to Plead Guilty," *Kansas City Star,* July 11, 1996, p. A1.
14. Joe Stephens, "Donor to Dole Is Fined, Confined," *Kansas City Star,* October 24, 1996, p. A1.

15. Judy Rakowsky, "Pair Admit They Lied about Haig War Chest; Falsified Data Boosted Campaign," *Boston Globe,* January 31, 1995, p. 18.

16. *Boston Globe,* "2 Who Aided Haig in '88 Sentenced," April 25, 1995, p. 25.

17. *Washington Post,* "FEC Imposes $40,000 Fine on Democratic Fund-Raiser," January 24, 1999, p. A7.

18. Butterfield, "Ex-Aide to Dole Campaign," p. B10.

19. PR Newswire, "Statement of Thomas E. Dwyer," October 23, 1996.

20. Butterfield, "Ex-Aide to Dole Campaign," p. B10.

21. Richard Sisk, "Bill No Fall Guy, but Rakes in Dough," *New York Daily News,* October 21, 1996, p. 6.

22. Howard Kurtz, *Spin Cycle: Inside the Clinton Propaganda Machine* (New York: Free Press, 1998).

23. Linda Greenhouse, "After 23 Years, Justices Will Revisit Campaign Limits," *New York Times,* January 26, 1999, p. A13.

24. Amy Keller, "Reed Plans Brief on Campaign Contributions," *Roll Call,* April 14, 1999.

25. Center for Responsive Politics, "Soft Money Special Release," February 4, 1998, World Wide Web address *http://www.crp.org.*

26. Adamany and Agree, *Political Money.*

CHAPTER 5

1. Dick Morris, *Behind the Oval Office* (New York: Random House, 1997).

2. Ibid., chapter 8.

3. Glenn Bunting, "Clinton's Hard and Fast Ride on Donation Trail," *Los Angeles Times,* December 22, 1997, p. A1.

4. Glenn Bunting and K. Connie Kang, "From Hero to Hot Potato," *Los Angeles Times,* October 19, 1996, p. A1, and Brian Duffy, "A Fund-Raiser's Rise and Fall," *Washington Post,* May 13, 1997, p. A1.

5. Bunting and Kang, "From Hero to Hot Potato," p. A1.
6. Tim Weiner and David Sanger, "Democrats Hoped to Raise $7 Million from Asians in U.S.," *New York Times,* December 28, 1996, p. 1.
7. Bunting and Kang, "From Hero to Hot Potato," p. A1.
8. Weiner and Sanger, "Democrats Hoped to Raise," p. 1.
9. Bunting and Kang, "From Hero to Hot Potato," p. A1.
10. Ruth Marcus and Charles Babcock, "Visit Spurred Indonesians' Gift, Says DNC," *Washington Post,* October 12, 1996, p. A21.
11. David Sanger and James Sterngold, "Fund-Raiser for Democrats Now Faces Harsh Spotlight," *New York Times,* October 21, 1996, p. A1.
12. William Clayton, Jr., "Both Parties Trade Accusations over Foreign Political Contributions," *Houston Chronicle,* October 21, 1996, p. 9.
13. Ibid.
14. John Harris, "President Sidesteps Funds Flap," *Washington Post,* October 22, 1996, p. A1.
15. Alan Miller, Glenn Bunting, and Maura Dolan, "$325,000 Gift to Democrats Raises New Set of Questions," *Los Angeles Times,* October 23, 1996, p. A1.
16. Weiner and Sanger, "Democrats Hoped to Raise," p. 1.
17. Glenn Bunting, "Records Show Wider Role on Asia for Fund-Raiser," *Los Angeles Times,* November 7, 1996, p. A1.
18. David Sanger, "President Admits He and Indonesian Had Policy Talks," *New York Times,* November 16, 1996, p. 1.
19. Weiner and Sanger, "Democrats Hoped to Raise," p. 1.
20. David Rosenbaum, "Senate Panel Is Told Huang Kept Ties to Company Linked to China," *New York Times,* July 16, 1997, p. A1.
21. Mark Gladstone and Marc Lacey, "Senate Probes Contacts Made by Huang," *Los Angeles Times,* July 18, 1997, p. A12.
22. Lena Sun, "Probe Fails to Link Huang, China Plan," *Washington Post,* July 20, 1997, p. A6.

NOTES TO PAGES 96–104

23. Bunting, "Clinton's Hard and Fast Ride," p. A1.
24. Ibid.
25. Ibid.
26. Ibid.
27. Ibid.
28. Robert Jackson and Ronald Ostrow, "Primary Target Charged in Probe of Clinton Donors," *Los Angeles Times,* July 14, 1998, p. A1.
29. Alan Miller and Ronald Ostrow, "Fund-Raiser Huang Aids Starr Case, Sources Say," *Los Angeles Times,* November 11, 1998, p. A15, and David Johnston, "Democratic Money Man Has Immunity from Starr," *New York Times,* November 11, 1998, p. A24.
30. Eliza Newlin Carney, "Pitfalls for the Probes," *National Journal,* May 17, 1997, pp. 991–992.
31. Jeff Gerth and Eric Schmitt, "House Panel Says Chinese Obtained U.S. Arms Secrets," *New York Times,* December 31, 1998, p. A1.
32. John Mintz, "China Aid Hurt U.S. Security, Panel Says," *Washington Post,* December 31, 1998, p. A1.
33. Paul Magnusson, "A Backlash against Beijing Is Building," *Business Week,* January 18, 1999, p. 55.
34. Ibid.
35. James Risen and Jeff Gerth, "China Stole Nuclear Secrets for Bombs, U.S. Aides Say," *New York Times,* March 6, 1999, p. 1.
36. Ibid. Also see James Risen, "White House Said to Ignore Evidence of China's Spying," *New York Times,* April 13, 1999, p. A14.
37. Walter Pincus, "Spy Suspect Fired at Los Alamos Lab," *Washington Post,* March 9, 1999, p. A1.
38. Jeff Gerth and Eric Schmitt, "Political Battle: What to Reveal on China Arms," *New York Times,* March 10, 1999, p. A1.
39. John Broder, "President Denies Ignoring Evidence of Nuclear Spying," *New York Times,* March 12, 1999, p. A1.
40. William Safire, "American Defeat," *New York Times,* March 8, 1999, p. A19.

41. Don Van Natta, Jr., "House Panel Subpoenas Democratic Fund-Raiser," *New York Times,* April 17, 1999, p. A11. This story was broken by William Rempel, Henry Weinstein, and Alan Miller in "Testimony Links Top China Official, Funds for Clinton," *Los Angeles Times,* April 4, 1999, p. 1. Also see David Johnston, "Committee Told of Beijing Cash for Democrats," *New York Times,* May 12, 1999, p. A1.
42. Jerry Seper, "PLA Is Tied to Campaign," *Washington Times National Weekly Edition,* April 12–18, 1999, p. 1.

CHAPTER 6

1. David Johnston, "Documents Cast New Light on Ickes's Tie to Teamsters," *New York Times,* October 7, 1998, p. A14.
2. Ronald Hrebenar and Ruth Scott, *Interest Group Politics in America,* 2nd ed. (Englewood Cliffs, N.J.: Prentice-Hall, 1990), pp. 35, 47.
3. Peter Kilborn, "California Strike Becomes a Battle over Permanent Job Replacements," *New York Times,* April 17, 1994, p. 22.
4. Mark Arax, "Strikers Reap Harvest of Bitterness," *Los Angeles Times,* May 10, 1994, p. A3.
5. Kilborn, "California Strike Becomes a Battle," p. 22.
6. Gavin Power, "Long Strike Spotlights Key Issue," *San Francisco Chronicle,* September 12, 1992, p. B1.
7. Bill Wallace, "Teamster Boss Says Reforms on Track," *San Francisco Chronicle,* October 21, 1992, p. A2.
8. Jeffrey Goldberg, "Jimmy Hoffa's Revenge," *New York Times Magazine,* February 8, 1998, p. 38.
9. Wallace, "Teamster Boss," p. A2.
10. Michael Doyle, "White House Accused of Pro-Union Bias," *Sacramento Bee,* November 17, 1993, p. D1.
11. Ibid.
12. Paul Schnitt, "NLRB Ruling Favors Striking Teamsters in Stockton," *Sacramento Bee,* January 24, 1995, p. D1.

13. Susan Schmidt, "Teamsters Contributions to Clinton Effort Probed," *Washington Post,* October 9, 1997, p. A1.

14. Ibid.

15. Ibid.

16. Bradley Stertz and Richard Ryan, "Teamsters and Politics: White House Memo: Help the Teamsters," *Detroit News,* October 21, 1997, p. A1.

17. Ibid.

18. Goldberg, "Jimmy Hoffa's Revenge," p. 38. Also see Steven Greenhouse, "Hoffa the Son Hopes to Put House in Order," *New York Times,* May 1, 1999, p. A9.

19. Roberto Suro, "Reno Orders Preliminary Ickes Probe," *Washington Post,* September 2, 1998, p. A1.

20. David Johnston, "Reno Orders Inquiry into Ickes's Testimony before Senate," *New York Times,* September 2, 1998, p. A20.

21. Ronald Ostrow and Alan Miller, "Reno Makes Ickes Possible Target of Probe," *Los Angeles Times,* September 2, 1998, p. A5.

22. Johnston, "Documents Cast New Light," p. A14.

23. Ibid.

24. Ibid., and Francis Clines, "A Point Man under Fire," *New York Times,* November 29, 1998, p. 46.

25. David Johnston, "Reno Delays Ruling on Special Prosecutor for Clinton Aide," *New York Times,* December 1, 1998, p. A22.

26. Johnston, "Reno Orders Inquiry," p. A20.

27. *Providence Journal,* "Attorney General Rejects Outside Probe of Ickes," January 30, 1999, p. A7.

28. David Johnston, "Reno Declares Ex-Clinton Aide Broke No Law," *New York Times,* January 30, 1999, p. A1.

29. Ibid.

30. David Goldstein, "Ads Knock Clinton's Stand on Liability Law," *Kansas City Star,* April 30, 1996, p. A2.

31. *Atlanta Constitution,* "Dole Allegedly Exerted Pressure to Blunt Probe of Kansas Oil Firm," March 24, 1996, p 16A.

32. Charles Babcock, "Elizabeth Dole's Fine Line between Charity, Politics," *Washington Post,* May 2, 1996, p. A1.
33. Darrell M. West and Burdett A. Loomis, *The Sound of Money: How Political Interests Get What They Want* (New York: W. W. Norton, 1998), p. 138.

CHAPTER 7

1. William Eaton, "Nicotine Study Suppressed, Waxman Says," *Los Angeles Times,* April 1, 1994, p. A20, and Philip Hilts, " '81 Tobacco Study Discussed Raising Levels of Nicotine," *New York Times,* April 14, 1994, p. A1.
2. Philip Hilts, "Tobacco Chiefs Say Cigarettes Aren't Addictive," *New York Times,* April 15, 1994, p. A1.
3. Ibid., and Marlene Cimons, "Cigarette Chiefs Steadfastly Deny Smoking Kills," *Los Angeles Times,* April 15, 1994, p. A1.
4. John Schwartz, "Tobacco Executives Deny Spiking Cigarettes," *Washington Post,* April 15, 1994, p. A1.
5. Carrick Mollenkamp, Adam Levy, Joseph Menn, and Jeffrey Rothfeder, *The People vs. Big Tobacco* (Princeton, N.J.: Bloomberg Press, 1998), p. 250.
6. Ibid.
7. Myron Levin, "Tobacco Case Marked by Series of Sound Bites," *Los Angeles Times,* July 16, 1996, p. D1.
8. Ibid.
9. Hunt Helm, "Blowing the Whistle on Big Tobacco," *Louisville Courier-Journal,* May 25, 1997, p. A1.
10. Sheryl Stolberg, "Defectors Helping to Crack Wall around Tobacco Firms," *Los Angeles Times,* April 3, 1996, p. A1.
11. *Washington Post Magazine,* "Where There's Smoke," December 3, 1995, p. W22.
12. Cimons, "Cigarette Chiefs Steadfastly Deny," p. A1. The figures on young persons, smoking, and death are cited in John Schwartz, "As Proposal Dies, Anger and Optimism," *Washington Post,* June 18, 1998, p. A18.

13. Hunt Helm, "Blowing the Whistle," p. A1.
14. Darrell M. West and Burdett A. Loomis, *The Sound of Money: How Political Interests Get What They Want* (New York: W. W. Norton, 1998), p. 49.
15. Ibid., p. 69.
16. Maria LaGanga and Ronald Brownstein, "Dole Revives Issue of Smoking's Effects," *Los Angeles Times,* July 3, 1996, p. A5.
17. West and Loomis, *The Sound of Money,* p. 50.
18. Gary Lee, "Cigarette Industry Has Ties to Both Campaigns," *Washington Post,* August 27, 1992, p. A29.
19. Jill Abramson with Barry Meier, "Tobacco Braced for Costly Fight," *New York Times,* December 15, 1997, p. A1.
20. Charles Babcock, "Congressmen Tee Off for Fun, Profit," *Washington Post,* January 26, 1989, p. A1. In addition, Big Tobacco kept prominent lawyers on retainer. Throughout the time he served as independent counsel, for example, Kenneth Starr represented Brown and Williamson. See Thomas Ferguson, "Smoke in Starr's Chamber," *Nation,* March 8, 1999, pp. 12–13, 14.
21. Mollenkamp et al., *The People vs. Big Tobacco,* p. 253.
22. Ibid., pp. 252–253.
23. LaGanga and Brownstein, "Dole Revives Issue," p. A5.
24. Ibid.
25. Anthony Flint, "Liggett Move Closes a Rift in Opposition," *Boston Globe,* March 25, 1997, p. A3.
26. Henry Weinstein and Myron Levin, "$368-Billion Tobacco Accord," *Los Angeles Times,* June 21, 1997, p. A1.
27. Ibid.
28. Ibid.
29. Jeffrey Goldberg, "Big Tobacco's Endgame," *New York Times Magazine,* June 21, 1998, p. 36.
30. Marc Fisher and John Schwartz, "Trying to Snuff Out the Tobacco Culture," *Washington Post,* June 22, 1997, p. A1.
31. John Schwartz, "Tobacco Negotiators Try to Bolster Deal," *Washington Post,* August 14, 1997, p. A13.

32. Weinstein and Levin, "$368-Billion Tobacco Accord," p. A1.
33. Fisher and Schwartz, "Trying to Snuff Out," p. A1.
34. Schwartz, "As Proposal Dies," p. A18.
35. Goldberg, "Big Tobacco's Endgame," p. 36.
36. Ibid.
37. Ibid.
38. National Public Radio, *All Things Considered,* May 19, 1998.
39. Goldberg, "Big Tobacco's Endgame," p. 36.
40. Wendy Koch, "Legislation's Defeat Has Effects beyond Tobacco," *USA Today,* June 18, 1998, p. 2A.
41. Ibid.
42. Thomas Ferguson, *Golden Rule: The Investment Theory of Party Competition and the Logic of Money-Driven Political Systems* (Chicago: University of Chicago Press, 1995).

CHAPTER 8

1. Ruth Marcus, "Foundation for Special Interests: Sen. Helms's Charity Gets Large Gifts from Taiwan, Kuwait, Tobacco," *Washington Post,* October 26, 1996, p. A1.
2. Ibid.
3. Ibid.
4. Linda Feldmann, "Taking Back the House," *Christian Science Monitor,* March 26, 1992, p. 6.
5. Charles Walston, "Gingrich Gets Boost from GOP Fund, but Aides Say PAC Not Helping Re-Election Bid," *Atlanta Constitution,* February 24, 1992, p. C3.
6. Mike Christensen, "Gingrich's PAC Enlarges His Realm," *Atlanta Constitution,* June 11, 1992, p. A1.
7. Charles Babcock, "PAC Ties to Gingrich Class Questioned," *Washington Post,* September 3, 1993, p. A1.
8. David Rosenbaum, "I.R.S. Clears a Foundation in Gingrich's Ethics Dispute," *New York Times,* February 4, 1999, p. A20.
9. Ibid.

10. Damon Chappie, "Gingrich Group May Avoid IRS Sanction," *Roll Call,* February 22, 1999, p. 1.
11. Damon Chappie, "IRS Revokes Tax-Exempt Status of Defunct Newt Group," *Roll Call,* March 15, 1999.
12. Ibid.
13. Jill Abramson and Leslie Wayne, "Both Parties Were Assisted by Non-Profit Groups in 1996," *New York Times,* October 24, 1997, p. A1.
14. Darrell M. West and Burdett A. Loomis, *The Sound of Money: How Political Interests Get What They Want* (New York: W. W. Norton, 1998).
15. Leslie Wayne, "Papers Detail G.O.P. Ties to Tax Group," *New York Times,* November 10, 1997, p. A27.
16. Ibid.
17. Juliet Eilperin and Jim VandeHei, "Newt's Ally Norquist Targets Labor, Lawyers," *Roll Call,* February 19, 1998, p. 1.
18. James Youngclaus, "Soft Money, Issue Ads, Non-Profits May Nationalize '98 Local Elections," *Capital Eye* (Washington, D.C.: Center for Responsive Politics), March 15, 1998, p. 4.
19. Abramson and Wayne, "Both Parties Were Assisted," p. A1.
20. Youngclaus, "Soft Money, Issue Ads," p. 4.
21. Abramson and Wayne, "Both Parties Were Assisted," p. A1.
22. Amy Keller, "Christian Coalition Probe Heats Up," *Roll Call,* February 18, 1999, p. 1.
23. Ibid.
24. Joel Bleifuss, "Taking Issue: Would Regulating Advocacy Ads Restrict Free Speech," *Capital Eye* (Washington, D.C.: Center for Responsive Politics), November 15, 1997, p. 1, and Richard Gephardt, "GOP Provides Payback to Secret Multi-Million Dollar Contributor," *Outrage of the Week* fax (Washington, D.C.: Democratic Policy Committee), October 31, 1997.
25. R. H. Melton, "Dole's Tax-Exempt Group Plans to Refund Millions," *Washington Post,* June 21, 1995, p. A1.

26. Ruth Marcus and Charles Babcock, "Alexander Raised Millions for TV Project," *Washington Post,* December 30, 1995, p. A1.

27. Douglas Frantz, "Populist Candidate Has Sophisticated and Lucrative Political Apparatus," *New York Times,* March 4, 1996, p. B8.

28. *San Diego Union-Tribune,* "Gore on the Griddle," August 27, 1998, p. B10.

29. Leslie Wayne and Christopher Drew, "G.O.P. Tool to Revive Party Instead Results in Scrutiny," *New York Times,* June 2, 1997, p. A17.

30. Ibid.

31. Nicholas Lemann, "Citizen 501 C(3)," *Atlantic Monthly,* February 1997, pp. 18–20.

32. Wayne and Drew, "G.O.P. Tool to Revive Party," p. A17.

33. Ibid.

34. David Johnston, "I.R.S. Redesigns Form on Tax-Exempt Status," *New York Times,* June 29, 1998, p. D4.

35. Damon Chappie, "The IRS's 'Story of M' May Affect '96 Politics," *Roll Call,* April 15, 1996, p. 1.

36. Ibid.

37. Damon Chappie, "Judge Denies Tax Exemption to All-GOP Group," *Roll Call,* March 9, 1998, p. 1.

38. Ibid.

39. David Johnston, "Court Rules against I.R.S. in Charity Case," *New York Times,* February 12, 1999, p. C1.

40. Damon Chappie, "North Group Loses IRS Ruling," *Roll Call,* March 22, 1999, p. 1.

41. Ibid.

42. Peter Slevin, "Judge Upholds IRS Action against Church That Sponsored Campaign Ad," *Washington Post,* March 31, 1999, p. A5. Also see Gustav Niebuhr, "Court Upholds I.R.S. Penalty for Church Ad in '92 Election," *New York Times,* April 1, 1999, p. A18, and Frank Murray, "Anti-Clinton Ads Cost a Church Its Tax-Exempt Status," *Washington Times National Weekly Edition,* April 5–11, 1999, p. 1.

43. Richard Stevenson, "Congress Sets Investigation of Tax Audits for Groups," *New York Times*, March 25, 1997, p. A16.
44. Ibid.
45. Guy Gugliotta, "GOP, Christian Right, and IRS," *Washington Post*, May 24, 1998, p. A5.
46. Ibid.
47. David Rosenbaum, "Tax-Exempt Status Rejected, Christian Coalition Regroups," *New York Times*, June 11, 1999, p. A18.
48. Gugliotta, "GOP, Christian Right, and IRS," p. A5.
49. Eliza Newlin Carney, "Stealth Bombers," *National Journal*, August 16, 1997, pp. 1640–1643.

CHAPTER 9

1. Herbert Alexander, *Financing Elections*, 4th ed. (Washington, D.C.: Congressional Quarterly Press, 1992).
2. David Adamany and George Agree, *Political Money* (Baltimore: Johns Hopkins University Press, 1975).
3. Eliza Newlin Carney, "Staking the Wrong Reform," *National Journal*, April 11, 1998, pp. 822–823.
4. Darrell M. West, *The Rise and Fall of the Media Establishment* (New York: Bedford/St. Martin's Press, forthcoming, 2000).
5. John Wright, *Interest Groups and Congress* (Boston: Allyn and Bacon, 1996).
6. Gary Jacobson, *Money in Congressional Elections* (New Haven, Conn.: Yale University Press, 1978).
7. Carney, "Staking the Wrong Reform," pp. 822–823.
8. Todd Purdum, "California Republican Tries Altering Campaign Finance," *New York Times*, March 25, 1999, p. A18.
9. Carney, "Staking the Wrong Reform," pp. 822–823.
10. Michael Malbin and Thomas Gais, *The Day after Reform* (Albany, N.Y.: Rockefeller Institute Press, 1998).
11. Richard Dunham, "Virginia Is for Lovers—of PACs," *Business Week*, April 12, 1999, p. 6.

12. Darrell M. West, *Air Wars: Television Advertising in Election Campaigns, 1952–1996,* 2nd ed. (Washington, D.C.: Congressional Quarterly Press, 1997).

13. Darrell M. West and Burdett A. Loomis, *The Sound of Money: How Political Interests Get What They Want* (New York: W. W. Norton, 1998).

Index

Chung, Johnny, 104–5
Church at Pierce Creek (New
York), 161
Citizen Action, 54
Citizens against Government
Waste, 162
Citizens for Reform, 152, 154–55,
186
Clinton, Bill: fundraising by, 6, 13,
36, 78, 84–106; impeachment of,
99–100, 104; issue ads support-
ing, 55, 80; opposition to, 6, 11–
12, 39–40, 43–51, 161; scandals
associated with, 57, 78, 87, 99–
106, 120; and Teamsters Union,
13, 106–8, 112–24; and tobacco
industry, 132, 140
Clinton, Hillary, 85, 87
"Clinton's Vision for a Better
America" (ad), 40, 43–51
The Coalition: Americans Working
for Real Change, 57
Committee for the Presidency, 28
Common Cause, 23, 157
Cone family, 155
Congress: investigations of Clinton
fundraising by, 93–96, 101–5,
115–20; post-Watergate campaign reforms passed by, 8, 19–
20, 70–71; public financing of
campaigns for, 180; and tobacco
industry, 13–14, 125–26, 128,
130–32, 136, 138–45
Connally, John, 9
Contract with America, 85
Cooke, Donald, Jr., 76–77

Corporations, 14, 123–24, 167–68,
187. *See also* Interest groups; *specific corporations*
Corruption (through campaign
financing), 7–8, 62–83, 172. *See
also* Cynicism; Money: laundering of; Secrecy
Couric, Katie, 137
Court rulings: on campaign contributions by individuals, 81–82;
effect of, on campaign abuses,
11, 59; on independent expenditures and issue advocacy, 86; on
tobacco companies' liability,
135–39, 141–42. *See also* Freedom of speech; Supreme Court;
specific cases
Covington and Burling, 133
Cox, Christopher, 101, 102
Cuff, William, 119–20
Cynicism, 7, 79, 82, 166–67, 169–
70, 173, 174–76, 189

D'Amato, Alfonse, 80
Davis, Martin, 117
DeBakey, Michael, 127, 128
Debates, 185–86
Democratic National Committee
(DNC): break-in at Watergate
headquarters of, 67–68; contributions to, 82, 98, 102; illegal
contributions to, 6, 12–13, 89–
94, 99, 104–6; independent
expenditures by, 36, 54, 55; issue
ads by, 80, 86; and Teamsters
Union, 116–18; use of nonprofits

Tournament Players Championship, 133
Triad Management Service, 155
Trie, Charlie Yah Lin, 95, 105
Turk, James C., 52
21st Century Freedom, 185
"Two-track" system of campaign
appeals. *See* Independent expenditures

United Cancer Council, 160
United States Tobacco, 146
U.S. Chamber of Commerce, 53
U.S. Justice Department, 75, 104,
120–22
U.S. Labor Department, 114
Uydess, Ian, 130

Van Buren, Martin, 16
Vote Now '96, 117, 152, 153

Walsh, Lawrence, 161
Wang Jun, 95
Washington Post, 68
Watergate scandal, 66–69, 79, 172;
effects of, on campaign reform,
8–10, 19–20, 64–65, 69–71,
168–69, 172, 190

Waxman, Henry, 126
"Weekend Passes" (ad), 26–28, 30,
32, 33–34, 80
Weldon, Curt, 103
White, Byron, 24
Whitewater land transactions
(Arkansas), 99, 100, 120
Wigand, Jeffrey, 129
Williams, Merrell, 129
Williams, Robin, 82
Williams, Roy, 109
Winfrey, Oprah, 28
Wingate College (North Carolina),
146
Winston Cup Series, 139
Wiriadinata, Arief and Soraya,
90–91
Woodward, Bob, 68
Worthen Bank (Little Rock, Arkan-
sas), 87–88
Wright, John, 177
Wyatt Tarrant and Combs, 129
Wynder, Ernst, 127

Young, Ambrose Tung, 158

Ziegler, Ron, 68

DATE DUE

			Printed in USA

HIGHSMITH #45230